Investigating Safely

Investigating Safely

A Guide for High School Teachers

By Juliana Texley, Terry Kwan, and John Summers

NATIONAL SCIENCE TEACHERS ASSOCIATION
Arlington, Virginia

NATIONAL SCIENCE TEACHERS ASSOCIATION

Claire Reinburg, Director
J. Andrew Cocke, Associate Editor
Judy Cusick, Associate Editor
Betty Smith, Associate Editor

ART AND DESIGN Linda Olliver, Director
    Shennen Bersani, Cover art
    Linda Olliver, Interior illustration
    Photo model for cover from *Chemistry with Computers,* published by Vernier Software and Technology
PRINTING AND PRODUCTION Catherine Lorrain-Hale, Director
    Nguyet Tran, Assistant Production Manager
    Jack Parker, Desktop Publishing Specialist
*sci*LINKS Tyson Brown, Manager
    David Anderson, Web and Development Coordinator

NATIONAL SCIENCE TEACHERS ASSOCIATION
Gerald F. Wheeler, Executive Director
David Beacom, Publisher

Library of Congress Cataloging-in-Publication Data
Kwan, Terry.
  Investigating safely : a guide for high school teachers / by Terry Kwan, Juliana Texley, and John Summers.
    p. cm.
  Includes bibliographical references and index.
  ISBN 0-87355-202-4
  1. Science—Study and teaching (Secondary school) 2. Science rooms and equipment—Safety measures. 3. Laboratories—Safety measures. I. Texley, Juliana. II. Summers, John, 1936- III. Title.
  Q181.K887 2004
  507'.1'273—dc22
                 2004003159

NSTA is committed to publishing quality material that promotes the best in inquiry-based science education. However, conditions of actual use may vary, and the safety procedures and practices described in this book are intended to serve only as a guide. Additional precautionary measures may be required. NSTA and the authors do not warrant or represent that the procedures and practices in this book meet any safety code or standard of federal, state, or local regulations. NSTA and the authors disclaim any liability for personal injury or damage to property arising out of or relating to the use of this book, to including any of the recommendations, instructions, or materials contained therein.

Featuring SciLinks®—a way to connect text and the Internet. Up-to-the-minute online content, classroom ideas, and other materials are just a click away. Go to page ix to learn more about this educational resource.

SCI LINKS.
THE WORLD'S A CLICK AWAY

Contents

Introduction

It has been many years since NSTA published a laboratory safety guide for high school teachers. Many things have changed. We have more to teach, and the concepts are more complex. Technology has permitted us to gather and transmit information with increasing speed. We have access to new research and data about toxicity of materials and dangers in methods that were not apparent years ago.

Social conditions have changed too. Today's teachers work with increasingly diverse student populations, including students with many special needs and sensitivities for whom they must design lab and field work. High-stakes tests have narrowed our focus and sharpened the scrutiny of our communities. The public is more litigious, increasing teachers' concerns about liability.

But today's students need hands-on experience in science more than ever. They need to observe and investigate, practicing the skills which will enable them to make good decisions and to work in the complex world of the twenty-first century.

The good news is that we now have information about alternatives and options that we never had before. We can still provide the investigative and observational activities that are essential to helping students understand the content and the methods of science. We can still set the scene for the discrepant events that produce the "Aha!" so essential to engendering true understanding and love of the scientific endeavor.

Teachers today can implement exciting curricula based on the National Science Education Standards in a safe learning environment if they have background knowledge and good sense. To do so requires planning and preparation, but it's well worth the effort.

This book is one of a series of three that are intended to offer positive options, even as they raise awareness of potential hazards: *Exploring Safely* is for elementary school teachers, and *Inquiring Safely* is the middle school volume. As we did in the first two volumes, we've included many anecdotes to highlight and reinforce ideas. Though we have changed the names and made some other modifications, all of the stories are based on actual events.

Although the traditional safety manual tends to be a compilation of safety rules, regulations, and lists, this book takes another path. We offer a more narrative style, providing discussions of safety concepts in the context of commonplace situations in real classrooms. We hope this approach makes these books enjoyable to read as well as valuable to reference. Because we recognize that another way to use the book is to look for specific topics, we have included a detailed index to help you locate the information you need. You will also find that some of the same information is repeated in several sections. This is to minimize flipping back and forth to find the information you need.

We also hope that the books are thought provoking. No single publication can cover every eventuality or all the specific policies and rules promulgated by federal, state, and local authorities. We encourage you to make connections and generalize from the ideas presented. Our goal is to provide you, the teacher, with examples of safe practices and to help you become more alert to ways of ensuring safety when you teach science in your classroom and in field studies. Above all, we encourage you to use common sense and stay up-to-date with district policies.

We believe that creating a safe environment for teaching and learning science is a group endeavor, led by the teacher, but joined by the entire school community. We have included information that we hope will be useful for you to share with supervisors and administrators so they fully understand the support they must provide to enable you to conduct a safe and effective science program. As you read this book, we hope it helps you "see" your physical environment and your procedures through a safety-conscious lens. In so doing, you will be able to give your students habits of mind that will last a lifetime.

Acknowledgments

Thanks to Betty Smith, our editor at NSTA, and to the contributors who provided advice and reviewed and added to this document: Stephen Barrasso, Jennifer Sischer-Mueller, Beverley Johns, James Kaufman, Nancy Lane, Ken Roy, Richard Silverman, Fred Wang, M.D., Sandra West, Victor Melehov, Victoria Augustine, Kathleen Conn, Lance Rudiger, Howard Schindler, Daryl Taylor, and David Vernier. Their tireless work has helped us polish our view of the classroom and enrich our offerings to you, the reader.

The authors have been working together for many years as part of the NSTA TAPESTRY grant program funded by Toyota Motor Sales, USA, Inc., and wish to acknowledge with thanks the generosity and support that Toyota has provided to hundreds of science educators and thousands of their students for more than a decade.

Author Biographies

Juliana Texley has taught all the sciences, K to 12, for 25 years and spent nine years as a school superintendent in Michigan. For 12 years she was editor of *The Science Teacher,* NSTA's journal for high school teachers, and served as an officer of the Association of Presidential Awardees in Science Teaching. She currently teaches college biology and technology and develops and instructs online courses for students and teachers.

Terry Kwan taught middle school science before becoming a science supervisor and teacher trainer. For the past 18 years, she has been an independent contractor, collaborating with private and public institutions to develop science programs, train teachers, and design science facilities. She served 18 years as an elected school board member in Brookline, Massachusetts, and currently serves as a lay member of the National Institutes of Health Recombinant DNA Advisory Committee and a community representative to Institutional Biosafety Committees for the Harvard Medical School and the Dana-Farber Cancer Institute.

John Summers taught environmental sciences, biology, and chemistry for many years and continues to be involved in programs to support teaching and learning of the sciences at the precollege level. A presenter at numerous NSTA and American Association for the Advancement of Science (AAAS) conferences, he is also a faculty member for online teacher training. He has served on panels to structure and review frameworks, assessments, and systemic initiatives in the state of Washington. His special interests include using science-oriented outdoor experiences to challenge and connect with at-risk students.

How can you and your students avoid searching hundreds of science websites to locate the best sources of information on a given topic? SciLinks, created and maintained by the National Science Teachers Association (NSTA), has the answer.

In a SciLinked text, such as this one, you'll find a logo and keyword near a concept your class is studying, a URL (*www.scilinks.org*), and a keyword code. Simply go to the SciLinks website, type in the code, and receive an annotated listing of as many as 15 Web pages—all of which have gone through an extensive review process conducted by a team of science educators. SciLinks is your best source of pertinent, trustworthy Internet links on subjects from astronomy to zoology.

Need more information? Take a tour—*http://www.scilinks.org/tour/*

Setting the Scene

Safer Science Is a Habit of Mind

High school students live life on the edge—almost ready to jump from school's carefully structured environment into college, career, and life. For each of those destinations, our students need a level of scientific literacy that includes caution and common sense. Each high school science classroom represents a unique set of challenges for the educators who seek to design a safe science program.

Investigating Safely

Developing a safe learning environment at the high school level is a great challenge. The subject matter is complex, the students are diverse, and the pressure for high achievement is intense. Through this guide we hope to help all those who care about secondary science achieve a new level of inquiry *and* safety.

In most professional libraries, you'll see one or more safety manuals. We hope you find that this book approaches safety differently. First and foremost, it is meant to provide teachers with the skills and self-confidence to increase the level of hands-on experiences in every classroom. While other books have compiled long lists of don'ts, we've tried to emphasize the dos. To that end, we've tried to emphasize guidelines rather than lists of specific hazards.

We have deliberately chosen to use an informal voice. The classroom experience from our three careers totals more than 75 years, but each week we learn new ideas about science and safety. We invite you to join in our community of learners, just as you would join us in a teacher's lounge discussion, to share insights and then to research on your own.

Share your insights with your fellow educators too. We've written these chapters not just for teachers but also for other members of the school community. The topics cover the entire environment, not just a select few laboratory experiences. Too often, a knowledgeable science teacher feels helpless to remedy safety hazards that other faculty members don't understand or appreciate. We've included material for administrators, special education personnel, paraprofessionals, and maintenance staffs.

Some guides emphasize how to shield students from dangerous demonstrations but forget the teacher behind the shield and the custodian who cleans up. We've emphasized safety for the entire school community. Administrators should take note of their obligations to their employees.

Read carefully, and you'll find yet another major difference in this safety guide. Our recommendations are based not only on physical dangers but also on developmental appropriateness. In many cases, we don't discuss just *how* to make an investigation safe, but also *why* it should or should not be done in the high school classroom. This information is not always comfortable and may be harder for veteran teachers to consider than for novices.

Like other guides, this one includes many disciplinary specifics. We have made a conscious effort to look not only at chemistry—the emphasis of most previous works—but also best practice in physics and in Earth, life, and environmental sciences. We've added specific new information on facilities and storage from NSTA and other expert groups. We've included tips on safety issues that arise when accommodating students with special needs and when moving science into the field and into the cyberworld.

We've included some key explanations and definitions in the Glossary on p. 187, which provides details on the way we use specific terms such as nonlatex gloves and prep rooms.

No safety book can be omniscient. No guide can prescribe every action or precaution that might be needed in a high school classroom. Safety is more than a set of rules: It's a state of mind. Because no single volume can anticipate everything that could go wrong, we believe teachers and administrators must make awareness of safety issues a skill and a habit. So we hope that as we share these experiences with you, you'll hone your own safety skills and that sixth sense that leads to an exciting and safe classroom for all students.

Using This Book

After you read this overview chapter, the way you use this book will depend upon your experience, your training, and your assignment. You may wish to skip right to your own discipline (in Chapters 5 through 8), or use the index to find best practice on a specific topic, such as Standard (Universal) Precautions, contact lenses, or Internet safety. Or you may use this book as a refresher for your own professional development, reading it from start to finish.

If you choose the latter course, you'll find some repetition. Some ideas deserve to be repeated. Some appear more than once for those who read only a part of the book, including administrators, support staff, and disciplinary specialists.

No matter what you choose to read, you are bound to find something that makes you uncomfortable—a treasured demonstration or customary practice that isn't considered safe. You're not alone. We've had the same experience in writing and working with teachers while developing the book. Change is never easy, but it's always educational.

The Adolescent Scientist

They walk into your classroom with cell phones and designer chic. They've never known a world that didn't have CDs, Windows, the Internet, or ATMs. Though they understand staccato rap and never miss a shot on MTV, it may be difficult for their teachers to penetrate that sophisticated veneer to make today's students understand important information on science and safety.

Teens have more experience with special effects and computer animation than authentic science investigations. So the first safety guideline for high school teachers is "Never assume." For students who may not be able to operate a manual can opener or a rotary-dial phone, commonsense precautions may be lacking. As you consider your program, develop a special set of eyes with which you can see potential hazards the way your high school students might experience them.

We must also recognize that our students come with widely diverse goals and interests. Our responsibility to provide a program that demystifies science and puts it in a safe and understandable context may well be even more important for students not planning careers in science and technology than for those who are. Safety instruction is a vital part of this instruction.

A Standard of Safety

The National Science Education Standards (NSES) (NRC 1996) leave no room for doubt. Inquiry-based science is vital to creating scientifically literate adults.

During the twentieth century, America's high schools grew. The number and kinds of courses increased each decade. To fill whole sections of calculus, Japanese IV, and advanced placement physics, economies of scale became the rule. Today's secondary teachers operate in bigger, more mechanized, more impersonal high schools with a greater diversity of students. Yet schools are challenged to create an individual educational experience for every learner. In Chapter 2, "Communities of Learners," we've discussed ways to modify instruction to increase safety for all of our students.

Many of our high school buildings are aging. National studies have found a significant increase in the number of buildings in serious need of repair, while unfunded mandates have left education with few extra dollars for renovation or expansion. Facilities are vital to safe science, as you will see in Chapter 3, "Where Science Happens," about space and equipment, and Chapter 4, "Finders Keepers," about storage.

Meanwhile, the body of content knowledge in each discipline of science constantly changes. What was yesterday's best practice can be today's unacceptable risk. Chapters 5 through 8 summarize many of the most common cautions in secondary science disciplines for teachers in life, Earth, and physical science classrooms. And, in Chapter 9, we've included tips for those times you can get out of the classroom and explore "The Great Outdoors."

Teachers have health and security concerns they would never have considered 10 years ago. To juggle all of the priorities of teaching science in the twenty-first century safely requires organization, preparation, and determination. Feeling overwhelmed already? You may want to skip to Chapter 10, "The Kitchen Sink." Having covered "everything" that falls into traditional safety categories, we've added a compendium of tips for school safety that go beyond the subject matter.

Our society today is more litigious, and more likely to blame teachers for factors that are beyond their control. So finally, in Chapter 11, we've borrowed from our favorite vision of the future to share tips on how professionals can "Live Long and Prosper" in the knowledge that their students are safe and scientifically literate.

Learning Never Ends

What does that degree on your wall mean? A prescribed sequence of courses? A statement of competency? A ticket to a job? Since your last formal course work, a great deal could have changed. An important step to safer secondary science is to keep on learning.

It's not just the content of science that changes but the standards for safe investigation. To structure a safe high school science program, teachers must be constantly in touch with current research findings. What's the latest list of banned chemicals? What new diseases might be spread in the classroom? What are the latest requirements for protective gear? Best practice is constantly changing. You must remain up-to-date.

In recent years, individual states have been changing certification requirements. Recognizing the need for constant professional renewal, few states grant permanent certification any more. Teachers know they must remain current to remain employed. Many teachers are working toward National Board Certification or state master teacher status. Unfortunately, safety training is rarely specified by states as part of required continuing education. But, without safety training, teachers may expose themselves and their districts to litigation and their students to unnecessary risk.

Students change too. Their interests and developmental levels are affected by previous school science experiences and by their experiences outside school. Demonstrations once considered motivational—like explosions—are now considered dangerously tempting to students who have been saturated with media violence. It's not enough to simply evaluate the content of an inquiry; you must also consider the context in which today's young scientists will receive it.

Ideally, science teachers would be certified—and safety trained—in multiple science disciplines. But they should instruct in no more than two distinctly different courses in any single year. Teaming several teachers who have been cross-trained but specialize in different disciplines brings together professionals who can support each other and create integrated courses that may be far more effective than single-discipline courses. Here's where the team approach is especially effective. You might ask for a content check from a teacher with a major in a discipline and a check on how appropriate the experience is developmentally from a learning specialist.

As a secondary teacher, you may be asked to join a vertical team with elementary and middle school teachers, too. Your responsibility there—to share content and to caution against inappropriate experiences—will be great.

You can't depend solely on the information that qualified you for your degree, your certificate, or the lesson plans in your file cabinet. You can't even depend on a book like this one for your safety knowledge base. Each disciplinary expert should assume responsibility for keeping up-to-date in his or her area. So this book has included Internet links and references for each chapter. We've also included information that leads you to online course work and mentoring by professional associations. We hope you'll join us as lifelong learners in the important endeavor of ensuring safety in science investigations.

The Schedule's the Thing

With the growth in size and complexity of schools came the assistance of computerized scheduling. Though this assistance may be a time-saver, it can also be a serious safety hazard in today's high school. The schedule can create inappropriate—and unsafe—combinations of students and classes. If the software is built around an algorithm that gives priority to minimizing conflicts and maximizing the number of students scheduled into the courses they want to take, safety may be forgotten.

Two of the most important safety priorities in a high school are the need to place similar preparations back-to-back and to limit the total number of students per teacher. That can inconvenience the football weight training program or the marching band, but this is a game for which science teachers must be the cheerleaders. Because lab chemicals and equipment must be set up in advance and must be secure when not in use, alternating between different sections in the same classroom without security problems is very difficult.

Computers can create unsafe combinations of students, particularly in smaller schools or in schools with "house" structures. Special needs students may be assigned together for remedial language arts or mathematics, where special help is available. But they can then, by default, end up clustered in one or two large science sections. A

Notes to Administrators: Scheduling a Safer Science Program

▶ Assign science rooms only to science teachers.

▶ Avoid assigning more than one teacher to each science room.

▶ Avoid assigning science teachers to more than one room.

▶ Schedule a teacher's sections of the same course to be run sequentially, with a prep period to allow cleanup and setup before a new course is taught.

▶ Provide secure locked storage for prepared science materials.

▶ Designate storerooms as close as possible to the laboratory to minimize moving materials through hallways.

▶ Schedule teacher prep time when the laboratory to be prepared is accessible and free of students, not in another room, a lounge, or a room that is in use.

▶ Avoid scheduling in which lab facilities are shared by several teachers whose science classes otherwise meet in nonlab lecture rooms.

science teacher could end up with more special needs students in a single section than a special education teacher could be legally assigned.

This is another problem that can be resolved if professionals are all on the same team. Computer scheduling is not an immutable force. You can, and should, advocate for hand-scheduling or manual overrides to ensure a safe and effective science program. There are also good strategies for staffing and program modification that can help when the schedule goes awry. Look for ideas in Chapter 2, "Communities of Learners."

The computer-generated schedule may also have to be modified to ensure that science teachers have access to their rooms to prepare safely for laboratory activities. Ideally, science teachers should be assigned their own rooms and have no more than two different preparations a day. If science rooms must be shared, they should be shared only with other science teachers. The potential hazards and the value of materials and equipment in a science room make its use by a nonscience teacher risky.

Realize that you *can* fight city hall and the automated scheduler. But it's easier if everyone is on the same team. Every commercial scheduling program *can* be manipulated to facilitate safe science. To make appropriate scheduling a priority of your administrative and counseling team, you may have to share information on safety, accidents, and liability with your scheduling team. If your principal is unaware of the safety risks associated with using science facilities for nonscience classes, you may need to point them out. If all else fails, remind your administrator of the 1981 legal precedent in *Bush v. Oscoda Area Schools*. In that case, a principal was charged with contributory negligence for scheduling a class in a poorly equipped classroom. See Chapter 11, "Live Long and Prosper," for tips on reducing liability.

As students move up our educational ladder, it sometimes seems there is less and less time for education. Interruptions—pep rallies, class pictures, college recruiters, even the ski club—seem to have precedence over your curriculum. Or do they? Work with your faculty, staff, and administration to reinforce the idea that interruptions aren't just a nuisance; they are a real liability to your program and a threat to safety. When interruptions are absolutely necessary, they should be preplanned and rotated. Share your safety concerns with the principal or headmaster.

The Best-Laid Plans

Whether you are a new teacher or a veteran, if you establish the discipline of preparing complete and detailed lesson plans, you will lower your stress and your liability. As you'll see in Chapter 11, these plans create not only peace of mind but also valuable documentation in case a problem ever occurs. But recognize that detailed lesson plans can look great on paper and fall short in practice. The best format is one that is convenient for you to prepare and easy for you to follow. You may want to make columns in your plan book to list materials to purchase, time requirements, chemical allocations, and safety reminders.

An important planning principle is that old lesson plans should not be reused without examination and evaluation. Even with revisions, do not keep a lesson plan beyond a set time—say, three or four years. When that time has elapsed, develop something new to ensure that your material is current and your teaching is fresh and enthusiastic.

You'll find some specific ideas for lesson plans in this book in sections called "The Savvy Science Teacher." You can find many more ideas in NSTA's journals, available online at *www.nsta.org*.

For Whom the Bell Tolls

Some high school periods are 48 minutes, some 55, and some schools alternate 90 or 120 minute blocks. Although longer periods are safer for high school science, a program can be modified for any schedule. The key is to plan like a general.

No matter what your time frame, it's guaranteed you will think the period is too short. To grab the extra minutes you need for safety issues and materials management, save time in other ways. Take attendance with a roster, a touch screen, or have

Making Every Minute Count

A Typical Lesson

- Overview and safety tips
  5 minutes
- Distribution of supplies
  5 minutes
- Activity period
  10 minutes
- Assessment break
  5 minutes
- Activity continues
  10 minutes
- Cleanup and equipment check
  10 minutes
- Brief review and inventory
  5 minutes

Total—50 minutes

students take a task card with their name on it. Have your safety review or quiz on a transparency or PowerPoint when students enter the room.

Notes can be taken and quizzes completed by the time you have recorded the day's absences. The faster you get down to business and complete housekeeping tasks, the better your class will run. A well-planned first five minutes sets the tone and standard for the rest of the class. This is just one good reason that science teachers need access to their rooms before the beginning of classes.

Find ways to automate and delegate certain tasks to students on a continuing or rotating basis. Individual students might be assigned to check in and check out equipment and supplies from specific counters or supply areas at the beginning and end of an activity. Consider adapting lower-school methods of organizing materials in specific positions so you can easily spot something missing in an open slot or shelf position.

Building in think time is also important. When students do a lab or other hands-on activity and then run out the door before they analyze what happened and why, they may not get much benefit from the lesson. That sometimes means preplanning to break lab experiences into smaller lessons, with discussion, journal, and cleanup time built in rather than trying to squeeze everything into a single period. Many teachers go through the motions of a potentially good lab, and then say, "Now, you see that we've proved …" A few blank looks, a bell, and suddenly you have lost any time for thoughtful analysis. If your lesson feels rushed, it probably is. Redesign the activity, expand it to multiple periods, build in self-reflection as homework, or find an alternative that permits you and your class enough time to think about the activity, not just complete it. All these time-savers have safety benefits as well.

Be sure that sufficient cleanup time is built into the activity and that all other work stops when it is time for cleanup. It's absolutely essential that you have time to inventory your equipment and make sure all spills have been cleaned up before the end of the period. Don't let your students crowd around a door waiting for the bell to ring—an invitation to theft, spills, and chaos.

CONSTRUCTIVE DEMONSTRATIONS

Demonstrations do not have to produce "shock and awe" to be motivational. In fact, an emotional reaction to a demonstration can actually interfere with thoughtful analysis. Use a discrepant event to challenge your students' thinking and initiate a lively discussion that supports constructivist learning. Consider these guidelines for safe demos (adapted from Flinn Scientific, Inc., *www.flinnsci.com*):

- Know the chemicals or materials you use and what will happen.

- Check all district, local, state, and federal regulations that might apply.

- Model appropriate safety precautions, including eye protection. Students need safety gear, also.

- Use minimum quantities of chemicals. (Use a video cam or projector to make the demo visible.)

- Don't risk body parts (tasting, touching).

- Have your fire and other emergency equipment available.

- Make sure you have all your documentation available.

Planning Lessons for the Safe Classroom

Once your schedule is crafted, your next challenge is lesson planning. No matter how standardized your state or district's program is, you still have many choices to make. One of the most important keys to a safe program is to choose classroom experiences with your students' developmental needs in mind.

A great thing about high school teaching is the experience your students bring to your classroom. Older students can relate to current events or practice authentic decision making in the context of societal issues that are important to them. But your students' air of maturity can be deceiving. In Piaget's terms, only about half of them will be able to use "formal reasoning" in most science contexts in high school. You will probably find that students are better able to apply formal reasoning in topics with which they have had a lot of hands-on practice in middle school than with topics with which they have had little or no direct experience. Always remember that these are high school students, who may look and behave maturely at times but in many respects are still very naïve and have an unjustified sense of invulnerability.

It's a natural tendency to bring some of the most exciting experiences from your own undergraduate

Just Say "No"

You have the responsibility to make sure every student understands safety instructions. That means you will have to say *no* to unnecessary hall passes, side trips, and absences. It may mean saying *no* to working on the yearbook and *no* to scheduling college-counseling appointments. It may mean that students who come in late and miss preparatory or safety instructions will be excluded from the laboratory investigation altogether and required to make up the work at a time convenient for you.

career into the classroom. But that can be a big mistake. Perhaps you have just attended a session for science teachers at a research facility and want to bring back to your students some current research science activities—create some labs. But consider where your students are in their intellectual development. Do they have the prerequisite understandings and the scientific foundations needed to grasp this current research? Your primary task is to provide that foundation. You grab a tool requiring careful and precise use, but they may see an object to be taken apart or casually brandished. You see an oxidation-reduction reaction; they see a bang that might impress a younger friend. Your students are almost adult—but not quite.

COPING WITH THE REVOLVING DOOR

▶ Greet students at the door looking for social and conversational clues that suggest interactions between students that may affect events in your class.

▶ Begin classes with a short activity that requires a specific product or outcome. Have instructions for the activity on the overhead or projector screen as students enter (e.g., a quiz on safety procedures associated with the lab or a list of supplies to gather).

▶ Suggest to students when and under what circumstances they might be able to leave class for an appointment that can't be scheduled at any other time (e.g., "You can leave immediately after cleanup if you make sure that someone gets you a copy of everyone else's data and you are prepared for the discussion of data that is scheduled for first thing tomorrow.").

▶ Make sure that fellow faculty and counselors understand the critical importance of safety instructions at the beginning of laboratory work and the special issues of safety and liability associated with science laboratory work. Ask that students not be pulled out of class during laboratory activities or, at the very least, never at the beginning of any lab.

▶ Exclude late students from lab activities until you are sure they have caught up with all safety instructions.

▶ Arrange credit for group responsibility. If a student joins the group midstream, ask the group to explain and document safety prep to the latecomer before proceeding.

The Teachable Moment

Many textbooks begin with a general chapter on safety. Teachers often follow this with a safety test, and keep the results as a record of the lesson. There's nothing wrong with a test. But this may be insufficient to ensure safe practice by students. The safety chapter is abstract and isolated from the activities to which the safety rules apply.

As with everything, safety lessons are best remembered when associated with real experiences. You should present general safety procedures—such as use of eye protection, decontamination, and hand washing—at the beginning of the course, but the best time to give specific safety instruction is in conjunction with a lesson or activity when the safety procedure is needed. Even though the procedure is one you may have reviewed a number of times, go over it again every time the activity you have planned requires the precaution. And don't forget the students who were absent or those who transfer into your classes. Ensure that every student has received introductory safety lessons as well as the safety instructions associated with each investigation, and document the fact in your plan book or calendar.

Say It Again, Sam

With a revolving door on their classrooms, high school teachers must be especially vigilant that every student has received all necessary safety instruction. Providing students with a written version of your instructions and safety directions and repeating them at the beginning of each class is important. When students are absent, they may miss safety directions. Keep an explicit record of what safety instruction has been given, when, and to which students. Keep this checklist as evidence that you gave proper and appropriate safety information to each student.

Homework Happens

Safety doesn't end when the bell rings, or when the school parking lot empties. You are responsible and can be held liable for assignments you give as homework. This includes independent study work and projects. Consider assignments carefully. Do not ask students to explore chemicals in their home cabinets or test soils from unknown grounds.

High school students are seldom supervised after school. In fact, many work long hours, squeezing homework into spare moments in random places. Your students' schedules should be considered as you assign homework. With some creativity, those part-time jobs that seem to get in the way of high school homework may be turned to your advantage. Sanitation requirements for fast-food restaurants or supermarkets, oil recycling rules for the service station, or statistical process control of a local manufacturer can become springboards for science lessons.

Physically Absent . . . Responsibly Present

Prepare appropriate plans for substitute teachers. If you direct a substitute to do an activity that results in an accident, you could be held liable, so if you are not certain that your substitute is fully qualified in your subject matter, do not have the substitute conduct laboratory activities. Many teachers prepare a special substitute folder for unexpected one-day absences. This folder contains instructions for nonlaboratory science activities that fit almost any part of the year. If you will be absent for an extended period, request a science-trained substitute and meet with the person to ensure that planned activities can be safely handled.

Your students can assume a great deal of responsibility when you are away if they are accustomed to sharing the routine of your classroom. It may also be possible to arrange for another teacher with the same assignment to supervise your lab while you are away and use the substitute to supervise his/her nonlab class work. Space limitations usually make it unwise to combine sections.

Students who are absent need to make up lab activities. High school students may ask for an extra credit assignment rather than complete a missed lab, but it is worth the effort to make sure that everyone completes lab work and works from the same experience base. Besides providing access to supplies and missed instructions, you must make sure the lab activity is completed under your direct supervision—never in a hall or storeroom. To make the process easier, organize materials in labeled boxes or bins containing the supplies and instructions for a particular activity or unit. Place a laminated card with the relevant safety rules in with the supplies. Although clear or translucent containers are ideal, shoe boxes and the 10-ream copy paper cartons may also serve you well. Create outside labels that not only show the title of the activity but also list the items inside.

The Parent Connection

Never assume that your students are so independent it is unnecessary to make contact with their parents. What's likely is that the parents want desperately to know what's happening in classes but get little or no information from their kids. If you have a newsletter, voice mail on your school phone, a website, or send out e-mail to parents, you might create a changing message: "This week's unit explores acids and bases ..." or "Parents, if your job requires sanitation or disinfection control, we may be able to use information from you to lend practical application to our lessons." If younger siblings are present, encourage students to work with parents to create a child-safe home.

A Reputation for Excellence—Teacher as Model

Your classroom should be a professional place where everyone will work seriously and dress appropriately. This is both for safety and for career preparation.

Model appropriate dress in your own attire—nothing baggy, torn, or hanging. Use eye protection when appropriate during your own demonstrations as well as whenever you require your students to wear eye protection. No food or drink in the lab applies to adults as well as students—no coffee or snacks, even in the back room if that back room is used for preps.

The physical environment can also contribute to or distract from the quality of instruction. Classroom clutter that cannot be distinguished from a midden both detracts from the seriousness of your endeavor and poses unnecessary safety hazards—fire, tripping, and undetected theft of valuable or hazardous materials.

Set High Expectations

As any veteran teacher knows, high achievement is the reward for setting high expectations for our students. This is as true for safety as for any other expectation. The more you make students responsible for using and enforcing safe laboratory and field-work procedures, the more easily safe practice can become habit.

High school science offers a rich curricular framework within which to build a safe environment for investigation. With help from peers, friends, and the wider scientific community, the future begins here.

THE SAVVY SCIENCE TEACHER

Older students may appear to be more sophisticated and mature than they actually are. Mr. H emphasizes simple, small-scale, and authentic experiences and never misses the opportunity to show his freshmen the application of science to everyday experiences. He directs his students' attention to phenomena they would never admit they don't understand:

▸ Boiling point? Challenge students to heat pure water in an open container to above 100°C. Many believe they can.

▸ Sublimation? Observe snow piles disappearing without creating a flood.

▶ Water pressure? Explain how a toilet works.

▶ Biochemistry? Find DNA oozing out of bananas and onions.

▶ Radioactivity? Start with smoke detectors in homes and radon in basements.

For Mr. H's students, the world just becomes curiouser and curiouser.

Connections

▶ American Association for the Advancement of Science. See *www.aaas.org*.

▶ American Chemical Society and ACS Board–Council Committee on Chemical Safety. 2001. *Chemical safety for teachers and their supervisors.* Washington, DC: ACS. Available in PDF format at *membership.acs.org/c/ccs/pubs/chemical_safety_manual.pdf*.

▶ *Flinn Scientific Catalog/Reference Manual.* 2002. Batavia, IL: Flinn Scientific, Inc. See *www.flinnsci.com*.

▶ Laboratory Safety Institute. James A. Kaufman, President. See *www. labsafety.org/about.htm*.

▶ MSDS for Infectious Substances, Health Canada. See *www.hc-sc.gc.ca/pphb-dgspsp/msds-ftss/index.html*.

▶ National Association of Biology Teachers. See *www.nabt.org*.

▶ National Board for Professional Teaching Standards. See *www.nbpts.org*.

▶ National Research Council. 1996. *National science education standards.* Washington, DC: National Academy Press. Online version at *www.nap.edu/books/0309053269/html/index.html*.

Communities of Learners

Promoting Science for Every Student

Just as the United States population has grown increasingly diverse, so has the population of our science classes. Our students bring a rich mix of abilities, learning styles, language, and cultural traditions to our classes. No longer tracked or shuttled to leveled course work, each member of our community of learners adds that adolescent zest for learning that enriches us all.

Science for All

The National Science Education Standards (NRC 1996) are meant for all students, regardless of learning style, background, ability, or aspirations. They encourage the highest achievement for every learner and place special value on diversity. While we move toward the realization of the Standards, high school classes must meet the needs and goals of an increasingly diverse student population. This places tremendous responsibility on science educators to find effective means of adapting instruction to the full range of students in their classes.

Science for all challenges our safety standards as well. As more students have been enrolled in laboratory science classes, older facilities have been stretched and awkwardly adapted to new uses. Former Earth science classrooms become the site of overflow sections of chemistry, and storeroom shelves become crowded. Besides sheer numbers, the facilities must accommodate older, larger students and students with physical disabilities.

Heterogeneous classes are often most challenging for veteran teachers, because their training was different. The more we find out about learning styles, the more we realize that the old methods of sorting students by ability or future plans are not only inappropriate but also ineffective. And the strategy of teaching to the middle with a few adaptations for the "slow" and the "gifted" will no longer work—if indeed it ever did. The wise teacher has seen changes in classroom composition as opportunities to enrich the curriculum and apply research to developing new and more effective instructional strategies that make science comprehensible to everyone.

Treasuring Diversity

A heterogeneous class has great value. The sensitivity students develop when they work in groups with students of differing abilities cannot be overestimated. This sensitivity to the gifts and needs of others is especially important in high school, where both social interaction and egocentric behavior are commonplace. The cooperation and teamwork skills students learn from communicating ideas in different ways are important for school and for work.

Structuring groups for safe science is an art in itself. Reading and writing are not the only skills required for success. To investigate, students must manipulate instruments, observe carefully, record accurately, and communicate among themselves. No single student will excel in all areas, and students who lag behind their peers in one skill can be quite advanced in another. By thoughtfully arranging lab partners or groups and monitoring and coaching these teams, you can create a situation in which students will appreciate each others' strengths and capitalize on differences in abilities to produce a whole greater than its individual parts. Insights and habits gained from these experiences in your class can be valuable assets in students' later lives on a job or in research.

There are challenges for our materials as well. It is rare that the textbook and other printed material from one program can accommodate all the students in a single course. It becomes the teacher's responsibility, with assistance from others, to find or prepare alternative or supplemental materials and ensure that everyone understands the key concepts of the course, directions for laboratory investigations, and safety precautions for all work. Large print, audio, or native-language support may be needed. Signage may also require review to ensure everyone understands it.

Though a large high school may have its drawbacks, there may also be the advantage of greater resources. Guidance counselors, school psychologists, English as a second language instructors, special education and learning disability specialists, school nurses, paraprofessionals, and administrators can help make adapting to diversity not only possible but practi-

SCiLINKS.
THE WORLD'S A CLICK AWAY
Topic: learners with disabilities
Go to: *www.scilinks.org*
Code: SHL16

cal. Remember that your subject, taught with a hands-on investigative approach, holds its own fascination and brings success within reach of a wide range of students. Set a goal of having every student succeed safely.

Least Restrictive Environments

Adapting programs for every learner is a serious legal and ethical obligation. It's one the science teacher may not avoid or pass on to other professionals. We are required by state and federal legislation to educate students in "least restrictive environments" (i.e., to the maximum extent appropriate with their nondisabled peers) and to reduce or eliminate physical barriers to everyone. That doesn't just mean giving disabled students a chance to take our classes, but creating a system that supports success. Only when our continuous, creative, and well-documented efforts at inclusion have been shown to be ineffective can we look at education in an alternative setting.

To many veteran teachers, inclusion may seem a burden. But it has distinct advantages for students and for teachers. Inclusion prompts us to look at our programs in ways that we otherwise might not have. Doing so has enabled many to achieve far more than anyone had ever thought possible and enriched our society as well.

A Good "IDEA"

The Individuals with Disabilities Education Act (IDEA, formerly PL 94-142, the Education for All Handicapped Children Act passed in 1975), reauthorized most recently in 1997, mandates that all students receive a free and appropriate public education regardless of the level or severity of their disabilities. A student qualifies for services under IDEA if he or she has a disability that interferes with learning. IDEA requires that, to the greatest extent possible, students with disabilities be educated with students who do not have disabilities. The law states that "unless a child's Individualized Education Plan (IEP) requires some other arrangement, the child is (to be) educated in the school which he or she would attend if not disabled [Section 121a.522(c)]." It permits the removal of the child from the regular classroom only when education in regular classes "with the use of supplementary aids and services cannot be achieved satisfactorily [Section 121a.550(2)]." This means that, if it is possible and practical for a student to learn a subject in a regular education classroom, it must happen that way.

There Must Be a Plan

Another mandate of IDEA is that beginning at age 14, and updated annually, there must be a statement of the student's transition service needs that focuses on his or her courses of study beginning at age 16—or younger if determined appropriate by the IEP team. That statement must include, when appropriate, a statement of the interagency responsibilities or any needed linkages. Of course, it would be great if every student had such a plan. But for a special education student, the plan is a required part of the legally mandated IEP.

The vocational plan may specify a sequence of courses or identify a specific set of skills to be acquired. When skills are listed in an IEP, there must also be an evaluation plan to track the acquisition of those skills on a continuum—separate from the more familiar grading system. As science teacher, you should familiarize yourself with the skill set identified for each of your students with an IEP. You could also work with the team to devise an appropriate evaluation plan that is practical for you and provides you, other instructors, the student, and the student's parents with meaningful information on the student's progress. Grading the special education student will also depend upon the contents of the IEP.

Alternatives to What Is Written

No student can be excluded from a course or an essential part of it based upon disability. If your course begins with a safety test, you may need to develop a different form for the language-disabled student, or you may need to enlist the help of a teacher consultant to verify that the student can understand and follow safety directions. You cannot simply exclude a learning-disabled student from an activity on the basis that he or she failed a particular safety test or quiz. You will also need to develop some remedial plan for instructing and testing those who would fail your regular assessment. Make safety evaluation a regular event, not just a September special. If a student fails to understand a written direction, you could be liable for an accident that occurs.

Accommodate, but Do Not Capitulate

You may have to redesign an activity so it can be safely performed by a special needs student or the class that includes him or her. Under IDEA, a student may not be disciplined if the behavior causing the discipline results from a disability. This provision means you may need to take special steps in planning laboratory activities, especially if there are students who are emotionally disturbed or present behavior problems. It is important to be aware of and plan for the behavioral limitations documented in your students' IEPs.

But this does not mean you have to tolerate unsafe behavior. It means that you may need to make a special effort to define the rules, set up shorter free periods, or limit access to certain types of supplies. It may require that you have a private discussion on behavior with the student and the student's special assistant. You may need to consider modifying assignments in cooperative groups. It may also mean that certain lab or field experiences are simply not appropriate for certain classes.

Science teachers should participate in the preparation of IEPs for their special education students and make sure that specific consequences for unsafe behaviors are embedded in the IEP. What will happen if that student fails to follow directions or endangers others in the classroom? If you consider using a resource room option for some experiences, be aware that conducting a laboratory in the special education classroom may have its own hazards. Students might be required to make up work with you, or you might request help to supervise the rest of the class while you work with a small group on a lab in a safer setting. Keep in mind that some activities may not be appropriate for some students. Recognize student limitations, and avoid placing students in situations with which they cannot cope.

Section 504 of the Rehabilitation Act of 1973 states specifically that no "otherwise qualified handicapped individual" shall be excluded from participation in a program or activity receiving federal financial assistance. That's another reason why we must use every means at our disposal to make sure that all students are involved in all activities in as normal a way as possible.

ADA—A General Education Responsibility

The Americans with Disabilities Act (ADA) of 1990 (*www.usdoj.gov/crt/ada/pubs/ada.txt*) prohibits discrimination against persons with disabilities. Like IDEA, this act mandates open access to regular educational facilities for people who are disabled. But ADA goes beyond special education. Where IDEA guides us in educating students working below their abilities, ADA guides us in providing access to our facilities and programs for all students as well as members of the community—teachers, parents, and members of the general public. A student may be academically gifted, and yet have a handicap that qualifies as a disability—attention deficit hyperactivity disorder (ADHD) is an example. A student with low ability may be functioning above his or her expected level and fail to qualify under IDEA but instead qualify under ADA. Physically handicapped students, even very high achievers, require accommodation under ADA.

Complying with ADA is a general education function. It differs from IDEA in several important aspects. An older building—or a private school receiving federal help—may not be handicapped accessible but under ADA may not need to be accessible until it is remodeled. People often refer to this as "grandfathering." But under IDEA, the entire program must be accessible (per the IEP) as soon as a special education student requires accommodations.

An ADA Checklist

- 86 cm aisles for wheelchairs with appropriate turning radii
- 70 cm of knee space
- A sink no higher than 86 cm and no deeper than 17 cm with paddle handles
- Paddle handles at sinks and on doors
- All entrances wider than 86 cm
- All flooring leveled or ramped
- A clear emergency exit through accessible doorways (avoid routes through automatic fire doors)
- Clear sight lines from a sitting position
- Locked storage
- No protruding cabinets
- Access to the safety shower
- Braille labels on safety equipment

Another twist to ADA involves disabilities such as ADHD. This disability *may* result in achievement gaps that would qualify a student under IDEA. But a high-achieving student whose ADHD behaviors create potentially dangerous activity in a science classroom may not qualify for special education yet may require accommodation under ADA.

Easier Said Than Done

Every state has its own regulations for implementing IDEA and ADA. Many of these regulations are more specific than the federal laws, but all are based on the same goals: to remove barriers and support achievement. Our communities of learners should be open to everyone. It's up to you to determine how this can be achieved in your curriculum and incumbent on you to request the support needed to make the student's experience safe and successful.

Both laws require the full cooperation of the administration. The science department chair and/or the district science supervisor may need to update central office administrators on how IDEA, ADA, and other legal mandates affect the science program and facility requirements.

If a student with a physical disability is assigned to your room, you should know all the details in advance. It is the school's responsibility to ensure you have all the equipment you need. That may mean different furnishings (see "An ADA Checklist," p. 19), Braille, text on tape, sound amplification equipment, earphones, personal word processors, or other assistive devices. You have the right to participate in formulating the IEP, and to request the help you need to modify your program and work space. Maintaining a good balance between order, accessibility, and open inquiry will take a great deal of time and effort, but it's always easier with a team. Don't forget you will have to spend time planning and preparing the support personnel (see Chapter 11, "A Diversity of Needs," p. 163).

A Special Set of Eyes

It takes a special set of eyes and ears to make sure your classroom doesn't present barriers to any budding scientist. Many professional preparation programs help by requiring prospective teachers to spend time in a wheelchair, on crutches, or with blurred vision or muffled hearing. The experience usually gives the teacher a very different perspective. The suggestions in this chapter do not cover every possible barrier, but they can provide your school team with a place to start. They are especially important if you are in an older building or adapted classrooms.

Begin your observations by looking at the physical facilities in which you teach science. Many high schoolers are full adult size, and most are probably still growing. Your facilities must be scaled to suit. To accommodate a student with a physical disability, you will need even more space—probably twice as much—and specialized equipment. A wheelchair may be as wide as 86 cm and may take up even more room if the wheels are cambered, or tilted out, for a paraplegic. Wall-mounted objects should not be higher than 86 cm from the floor, and there should be at least 70 cm of knee space under the desks. Many people with disabilities must sit on special cushions to prevent pressure sores. This increases knee space requirements. Sinks must not be more than 17 cm deep and must have paddle handles to accommodate people for whom turning knobs would be a problem.

The floor must be flat, including the path to the safety shower, and there should be no barriers such as taped-down wires or uneven carpet/tile interfaces. Make sure there is a good clear exit path from the room in case of fire. Don't rely on a route through a fire door that may close automatically if the fire alarm sounds.

Think about visually impaired students as you inspect your room. You may need Braille labels. Wall-mounted units should be placed above base cabinets. There should be no protruding edges or corners on casework and furnishings, an accommodation for visually impaired students that is valuable for everyone. You should also be conscious of acids, glues, or solvents that can make fingertips lose their sensitivity, a problem for students who read Braille.

Think also about students with hearing impairments, even minimal or frequency-limited disabilities. Allergies and overuse of loud speakers can cause temporary hearing disabilities, too. Learn to distinguish between unnecessary noise and the good noise of organized bustling. If class changes occur during your period, consider extra insulation over the door or window. Investigate sound-muffling wall coverings. And watch your own voice. You can cause yourself permanent damage by shouting above the fray. Insist on a businesslike silence when you need to provide instruction.

In designing a new facility, architects should be familiar with the requirements of ADA and IDEA and design accordingly. But you won't have any grace period under IDEA if a student with a physical disability is enrolled in your course. You must create an immediate plan for changes when a special education student or a student with a disability needs access. So, until a major remodeling project occurs, you will probably need to add portable lab stations, adjustable-height tables, and alternative sink stations.

SIGNAL VS. NOISE

Increasing the loudness of speech does not necessarily make it more easily understood by the hard of hearing. Raising the signal in relationship to noise (S/N, or signal-to-noise ratio) can be more important than raising your voice. The signal is the sound the listener is attempting to hear or distinguish. The noise is the ambient noise in the room. For speech to be heard clearly, the sound to be heard must be loud as compared to other noise such as side conversations, the whir of ventilation fans, and the hum of machines. This is the idea behind the use of FM amplification systems. The teacher's speech is picked up by a microphone on the teacher's lapel and delivered amplified directly to the student's earpiece so, to the student, the teacher's voice sounds louder than the ambient noise.

Different Strokes

In every high school, many students have what might be called undocumented social handicaps. Some are chronically absent because of low family support or high family responsibility. Some are virtually homeless, moving from friend to friend, while others find gang structure the closest thing to a family. Substance abuse can create behaviors that look much like attention deficit disorders. The relationship problems that can beset high school students can be overwhelming. There are even high achievers with so many leadership and extracurricular responsibilities that they're frequently absent, late, or leaving early from class. The side effects of what's happening in your students' world can affect the function of your classroom, causing not only distractions but also real safety problems.

With your sensitive "teacher antennae," you have to distinguish true social crises from the constant buzz of high school sociology. Is that junior in the back of the room crying because her boyfriend didn't say hello in the hall, or might she be pregnant? Science teachers often hear more than others because of the structure of their lab groups. It's important to know when to say "Get down to business," and when to carve out vital time to resolve pressing issues and ask for help.

Whether the reason is social or medical or stems from years of low achievement, some high school students have a low sense of fate control. In the words of the late science educator Mary Budd Rowe, they are "dice players"—believing that what happens to them in school occurs by chance rather than because of their own actions. Dice players think that teachers make up grades and that better achievement is out of their control. Low achievers often can't plan beyond today or tomorrow. For all of these problems, it's important to have a tight, consistent, and transparent grading structure. Have a system that encourages students to check their own progress at frequent intervals. Grade for small, short-term achievements because many students can't guide today's behavior based upon a potential grade a week away. And always reinforce the idea that success is within a student's reach, because those who give up are the ones most likely to cause real problems.

Limited English

If your class includes students with limited English ability, you should have safety signage that uses universally understood symbols and/or is in the native languages of these students. For students who receive English as a Second Language (ESL) support, make sure that the ESL instructor is prepared to assist with safety instructions. Identify other students who may be able to assist in translation, and ask the administration to hand schedule so that these students can be together and you can have communications support.

To Everyone's Good Health

Although high school students seem to find dozens of reasons to miss class, the presence of a cold or other infectious disease usually misses their list. Science class might be an ideal time to make clear that infectious disease transfers and that students need to stay out of school and away from others while infectious.

Allergies may sound like colds, but they persist and aren't infectious. The hygiene rules for coughs and colds apply to allergy symptoms, however, because infections can take hold in allergy-inflamed tissues. Be aware of the possible presence of allergens in your room. Check student health records early in the year to familiarize yourself with students who have allergies, and make sure that things you keep around your classroom do not exacerbate allergies. See Chapters 5, p. 68, and 10 "Persistent Problems," p. 139, for more information about allergens. Remember that allergic reactions can become life-threatening conditions very quickly. If a student develops hives or any sign of respiratory distress, call for medical help immediately.

Fighting Infection

- Teach basic health precautions as part of your curriculum.
- Send students with serious symptoms to the office or call the nurse or medical support system.
- Keep tissues handy and reinforce use and proper disposal.
- Keep soap near the sink and encourage hand washing.
- Do not allow students to keep stocks of nonprescription drugs in their lockers or dispense them to each other. (Many high school students carry a few aspirin or ibuprofen. Do not become involved in exchange of these items.)
- Ask that your room be kept relatively cool.
- Keep nonlatex gloves handy.

Be conscious of the possibility of diseases transmitted via blood and other body fluids. For information on Standard (Universal) Precautions, see Chapter 10, p. 142.

Do not provide medication—prescription or over-the-counter—to any student. Even the most common over-the-counter medication can cause a severe reaction. Never administer medicine of any kind. You are not qualified, authorized, or insured to do so. Discourage the practice of students' bringing their own medications to school unless a physician prescribes their specific use during the school day. If a student must have medication at school, it should be in an original prescription bottle labeled with the student's name and physician directions and kept in the school office or nurse's office under lock and key. Medication should be administered in the office in the presence of a trained professional. Students should not be permitted to store medication in their desks, lockers, or other personal storage area.

Teachers should also learn to recognize the signs of substance abuse—actual use and the signs of long-term damage after use. High school students who are chronically sleepy or lethargic may be working too many hours or may be abusing drugs. Those who can't seem to sit still may have attention deficit hyperactivity disorder or may be coming off the effects of drug experimentation. Whatever the cause, they may not be able to follow safety directions in your classroom. That's when the counseling office is invaluable.

A Little Help from Your Friends

Many schools are encouraging the use of coteachers to support the inclusion of special needs students in the regular education classroom. These additional adults can be a tremendous help and a valued safety measure. The arrangements are generally safer than scheduling a special education science class in another, less appropriate classroom. But the regular teacher must take a great deal of responsibility to make the partnership work effectively.

Coteachers may not have the preparation for teaching science, but they should have special skills in assessment, specialized instruction, behavior modification, and remedial reading that can help special needs students succeed in science. Treat your coteacher as a partner. Plan jointly, and alternate the role of lead teacher. Your coteacher may have more training in reading in the content area or test preparation. It takes continuing in-depth conversation for a coteaching relationship to work well.

When setting up a coteaching classroom, be wary of opportunistic scheduling. When a coteacher is assigned to a heterogeneous class, it is to support a specific special education student or students whose requirements are described in IEPs. But in some schools, other students with mild to severe behavior problems are added to the same section just because two teachers are available. This is unfair to the special education students and to the teachers. There is a synergistic effect when too many students with behavioral difficulties are assigned to the same section. Heterogeneity means there should be a good mix in every section. Also remember that even though the student-teacher ratio may be low in a cotaught classroom, the space guidelines for safety (see Chapter 3, p. 28) won't change, so your room may be too crowded for safe science.

THE SAVVY SCIENCE TEACHER

In late spring, Ms. L learned that the following school year, a student using a wheelchair would be enrolled in her sophomore biology class. Ms. L wondered how that would affect her program that included field trips to sample water from two local streams three times during the year.

The first thing Ms. L did was ask to participate in the IEP planning meetings for the student. As part of the IEP preparation, two members of the special education team accompanied Ms. L to the field sites. They recommended shifting one of the collection locations about a half mile upriver where a visitor's platform extended close to the riverbank and that an aide accompany the student on each field trip. The district's occupational therapist took several pieces of the sampling equipment and modified them with a variety of extension devices that would enable the student to participate in some of the collection studies. She also prepared a lapboard with special clamps and lips that would allow the student to test samples other students collected.

Once the entire class roster was available, Ms. L placed the student who used a wheelchair in a group with two students who had participated in the district's peer leadership program. That group produced some of the finest work in the class. By the end of the year, everyone had a great sense of accomplishment, and Ms. L wrote an article about her experience that was published in the state science teachers' newsletter.

Connections

▶ ADA, The Americans with Disabilities Act. See *www. usdoj.gov/crt/ada/ adahom1.htm.* and *www. usdoj.gov/crt/ada/pubs/ ada.txt.*

▶ American Chemical Society. 2001, 4th ed. Teaching chemistry to students with disabilities. Washington, DC: ACS. Available online *at membership.acs.org/C/ cwd/teachchem4.pdf* or in print.

▶ CEC, The Council for Exceptional Children. See *www.cec.sped.org.*

▶ IDEA, Individuals with Disabilities Education Act. See *www.ed.gov/offices/ OSERS/Policy/IDEA/ index.html* and *www4. law.cornell.edu/uscode/ 20/1400.html.*

▶ West Virginia University, Inclusion in Science Education for Students with Disabilities. See *www. as.wvu.edu/~scidis.*

Where Science Happens

Equip Your Lab for Safety

High schools stand at the hearts of their neighborhoods, and the buildings themselves may be among the community's biggest investments. Many of our nation's high schools have housed generations of teachers and learners, weathered enrollment ups and downs, and silently borne myriad changes in educational practice. But, alas, as times have changed many have not had the benefit of the modernization and expansion needed to support best practice. Even when there is plenty of space for science classes, the facilities may be far from adequate to support investigative programs safely.

The Practice of Science

The science disciplines encompass both content and practice. We know that a full understanding of science can be acquired only if students participate in the physical practice of investigation—observing phenomena, isolating and manipulating variables, gathering data, and critiquing and analyzing results. This requires physical facilities—space, furnishings, and equipment—that support safe experimentation. Even the best teacher, with the most advanced skills, cannot make science happen safely without the appropriate physical space. In the wrong facilities, science investigation poses serious safety hazards.

Each high school is a little different. Some traditional rooms were designed with lecture (direct instruction) in mind. Others have laboratories, or combination lecture and lab spaces. In years past, a popular practice was to assign science classes to regular classrooms for lecture and discussion on a daily basis and then schedule a single or double period lab once a week in a science laboratory. This system may be less expensive but is counter to what we know about a good science curriculum. Laboratory activities may not last an entire period and should be interspersed with discussions and direct instruction. Class discussions should give rise to many opportunities for impromptu rechecking of observations or investigation of new theories. Some investigational work should occur almost every day—so every science room should be equipped for safe laboratory investigation and every class session should be scheduled in a science room.

Take Out Your Tape Measure

To support high school science, the ideal room should have:

▶ a minimum of 4 m² per student (96 m² for a class of 24) for a laboratory, 5 m² for a laboratory/lecture room

▶ additional and specialized space to accommodate students with disabilities

▶ 1.4 m² for each desktop computer station

▶ 0.9 m² per student of preparation space for the teacher

▶ 1 m² of lockable storage area for every student in the room

▶ a ceiling height of 3 m

▶ two escape routes (a second door or large window without screen)

▶ ventilation of at least five (eight changes are now recommended) air changes per hour, with fume hoods for every chemistry or biology laboratory group

▶ hot and cold running water with soap

▶ eyewash facilities with tepid water

▶ fire protection

Source: Biehle, J., L. Motz, and S. West. 1999. *NSTA Guide to School Science Facilities*. Arlington, VA: National Science Teachers Association.

For simplicity, we've referred to all the varied spaces in which we teach as "science rooms."

Government studies have indicated that as many as one-third of America's schools need extensive renovation or replacement. Older buildings may have been built for different student populations or completely different curricula. Even new facilities can be too crowded or architecturally unsuited for science exploration. Science rooms specifically designed for chemistry, biology, physics, or Earth and space science sometimes end up in the wrong place or in the wrong quantity when large populations are subdivided by "houses," when curricula change, or when students with physical disabilities need accommodations.

The best new schools are built with the assumption that change will happen. For tomorrow's science, experts design science rooms that can accommodate any secondary science class. They try to ensure that space and utilities will be adequate, fundamental safety equipment will be present, and furnishings will be sturdy but flexible. But, in most cases, there is much that we can do to improve science rooms even without major renovation.

Give Me Space, Lots of Space

The single most important safety factor is space. Ensuring sufficient space in the science room is critical to supporting a safe program. With enough room, a small spill is just a cleanup issue. Crowded, the same spill can cause multiple injuries. Where students are clustered too closely, elbows knock into one another's setups, electrical cords are pulled from receptacles, equipment falls, and tensions mount. Check the accompanying box for minimal space requirements recommended by the National Science Teachers Association. Other professional associations may have slightly different recommendations, but most are similar.

A related factor is class size. Even with ade
space per student, total enrollment in a section
to be limited. Ideally, science classes should ha
more than 24 students even if the space might ac
modate more. Research data shows that accident
dramatically as class enrollments exceed 24. If
rooms are small, enrollment should be limited
further. The addition of an aide or coteacher ma
help—and may actually hurt—an overenrollme
tight space problem, because the aide takes up
and may not be well trained. When either spac
student goes down or class size goes up, the acc
rate goes up.

If you cannot expand space or limit enrollment to the recommended standards, then you must document the specific labs and program elements that you cannot do safely, notify the appropriate administrators, and, most important, *eliminate those activities that cannot be performed safely in the conditions you have.* Remember that notifying an administrator that an activity is dangerous provides written proof that you know a situation is unsafe. The responsibility to avoid the unsafe situation is yours—as is the liability if you do not.

in an impasse, don't hesitate to be proactive in seeking advice from your administrator.

A Room of One's Own

Ideally, each science teacher should have his or her own room with storage rooms and preparation areas adjacent to it. If rooms must be shared, they should be shared only with other science teachers and scheduled so that each science teacher can have access for setup when classes are not being conducted.

Teaching science in a nonlab room isn't just poor education, it is also unsafe. If a science teacher sets up labs and then has to teach elsewhere, the equipment and materials in the lab may be unsupervised or, worse yet, subject to tampering by other classes. A rushed teacher, dispensing lab equipment on the fly, is likely to make mistakes. Students who must make up work may end up without an appropriate facility in which to work.

If a science class must be scheduled in a room not originally designed for laboratory work, then lockable storage, hot and cold running water, and safety equipment are an absolute minimum that must be provided.

THE ART OF PEACEFUL COEXISTENCE

Sharing space, storage, and supplies is reality. Even if you have your own exclusively assigned classroom, you will, no doubt, share other spaces or items with colleagues. Cooperating with each other is not a matter just of courtesy; it is also a matter of safety.

▶ Recognize that all who share a room or space may share liability if something goes wrong.

▶ Establish and write a clear set of ground rules for use of the shared space that must be followed by all who use the space. For example:

  ▶ All entry doors and lockable storage must be locked upon departure.

  ▶ No students may be present unsupervised in any science room.

  ▶ All work surfaces must be cleaned and dried before departure.

  ▶ Storage of ongoing projects may only be in designated areas and may not include any fragile or hazardous materials.

  ▶ Storage of any chemicals must be accompanied by material safety data sheets (MSDS) filed in notebooks located in the main office and in the storage room.

▶ A designated bulletin area should be provided for written notes to all other users about any unusual conditions.

▶ No students may be present in any science stockroom at any time for any reason.

▶ Keep a set of the rules and a copy of this book in a location regularly accessed by all staff who use the shared space.

▶ Involve the department chairperson or designated administrator in establishing and enforcing rules for shared spaces, including shared storage and preparation areas.

▶ Request professional development safety training for all staff working in science areas.

If a colleague allows a student into the chemical storeroom, and that student removes the stock bottle of some reagent you ordered, could you be liable for harm that may result? It would be better not to have to find out.

A Lab for All Sciences

Should a classroom for biology be designed and built differently than a classroom that supports chemistry? For contemporary science curricula, the best answer is *no*. In high school instruction as well as in research laboratories, the fundamental elements of a safe facility are the same. Although physical science equipment may be longer, wider, and heavier than equipment for other sciences, and biology teachers may need microscopes while chemistry teachers have more use for spectrometers, all teachers need emergency equipment, eyewashes, showers, protective eyewear, clear and level counter space, secure storage, prep facilities, direct outside air ventilation, hot and cold running water, adequate utility services, and good lighting.

Course selections will vary from year to year, curricula and graduation requirements will certainly continue to change, and the separation between science disciplines will become less distinct. In the long run, the most effective way to accommodate a full investigative science program is to equip all science rooms for safe laboratory work and vary the furnishings to suit the discipline.

Floor Plans and Floors

A floor plan that distributes workstations as far apart as possible on perimeter walls has several advantages. Properly designed, each standing-height workstation with sink, water, gas, electric, and telecommunications service can support two lab groups working at countertops on each side of the services, so six such stations can accommodate 24 students working in pairs. Perimeter workstations maximize separation between lab groups and have students facing away from one another, which minimizes distraction and interactions between groups. Accidental sprays or spills are more likely to hit walls or windows rather than another working group. If you choose additional sturdy but moveable tables that are the same height as perimeter counters, you can extend work areas into the middle of the room when needed but maintain clear space and flexibility to accommodate activities from many different science disciplines. The tables can also be rearranged for discussion or lecture.

Older-style floor plans with large lab benches taking up most of the floor space in the room are much less flexible—specifically for chemistry or physics—and do not lend themselves easily to class discussions and large group instruction, necessitating separate lecture areas. In some cases, the lab benches create work areas that do not have clear, straight paths to exits and safety equipment. Students, especially those with mobility problems, could be trapped or seriously slowed down in case of fire or accident. If you must place workstations in the middle of the room, try to have compact service islands incorporating sink, water, gas, electrical, and telecommunications service, and use moveable tables that can be pulled up to the service islands in a variety of configurations.

The flooring itself can be a safety issue. Carpeting is inappropriate in general and should not be used for science rooms at all (see Chapter 10, p. 140). In older buildings, wood flooring may still be in place. This should be replaced in any renovation, with attention given to identifying and removing any hazardous material—such as elemental mercury from broken thermometers—that may have fallen between floor boards and remained in subflooring. Seamless chemical-resistant cushioned flooring works best. Sometimes this is installed in sheets, sometimes it is poured over a prepared surface. Two other factors should be considered. Flooring applied directly over a concrete base without some cushioning can cause fatigue and impact-related foot/leg problems. Flooring that is too shiny and smooth can be dangerously slippery when wet.

In the Room Where You Live

Take a few minutes to look around at your classroom with the objective eye of a visiting safety expert seeing it for the first time. Can you supervise every area where students may be working? If not, consider rearranging your furniture and adding strategically placed mirrors. Can students get to the sink or eyewash within 10 seconds? If not, eliminate some of the furniture. Do you have stores of junk? Teachers can be pack rats. Even the most spacious classrooms can be made unsafe by clutter you have accumulated over the years. Scan your favorite exercises onto a CD-ROM, and get rid of the paper.

Packing Relief

Having to pack up and move to another room may be the opportunity of a lifetime. Be ruthless. Do not pack and move anything you can do without. Do not seal any cartons with items you have not subjected to hard scrutiny—less is better. If you don't have time to look it over now, you probably never will.

Do not block escape routes or routes to safety showers and eyewash stations. Come in early one morning and conduct an imaginary emergency drill. In case of fire, is there enough room to stop, drop, and roll? Could everyone get out quickly? Remember that a fire door could close automatically, slowing down a disabled student. In case of an accidental spill, can students back out of the way of the splash or clear the area? If a splash should occur at any of the work areas, is there a quick clear path to a sink, safety shower, or eyewash? Make sure your escape routes are freely and easily accessible—not just unblocked, but realistic and immediate ways to safety for every person who may be in the room.

Water, Water, Everywhere

Every science room needs potable hot and cold running water. Hot water is needed for sanitation, hygiene, and general cleanup. Hand washing is required for the vast majority of science activities. In addition to its use in laboratory investigations, tepid water is needed for the eyewash and the safety shower.

Six sink stations installed around the room work well for 24 students. The sinks should be deep enough so that chemicals don't splash. At least one sink in each room should be wheelchair accessible and have paddle-handled faucets that can be operated with a closed fist.

Faucets can be a real maintenance headache. Better-designed faucets are solid, one piece, and secured directly into the counter. Avoid the more common and inexpensive types of faucets that have a separate gooseneck that can be unscrewed easily—and therefore wiggled loose or taken apart during class. Building codes may also require that faucets prevent accidental backflow from the laboratory station into the public water supply. If you need jet-spray nozzles, make sure that they are removable and that you remove them when they are not absolutely necessary.

In many states, water coming from science labs must pass through acid traps or neutralizing tanks before entering the regular wastewater system. Even if they are not required by code or regulation, you should consider specifying corrosion-resistant pipes and acid-neutralization tanks. If you have acid-neutralization tanks, remember that the marble chips in the tanks must be changed regularly. The frequency of this change is dependent on the volume and concentration of acids that run through the tanks, but in general change them at least every six months.

EYEWASHES

You need a plumbed eyewash that anyone working in the laboratory can reach within 10 seconds. The eyewash should be no more than a meter above the floor and accessible to people who use wheelchairs. The eyewash should have a flow rate of 3 gallons per minute, turn on with a single motion, and operate hands-free. It must be capable of washing both eyes simultaneously.

Bottled eyewashes are not recommended, because they do not provide enough water, and they can become a reservoir for dangerous microbes. All eyewashes should be flushed for two to three minutes every week. That helps protect against contamination by *Acanthamoeba*, a protist that lives in water and can cause serious eye infections.

In case of accident, the eyewash should be used to flush the eyes continuously for at least 15 minutes. Students should be trained to lift their eyelids away from the surface of the eyeball when flushing.

EMERGENCY SHOWERS

Every science room needs an emergency shower. This is essential for fire as well as for chemical spills. The shower should be 2 to 2.5 m above the floor, but the handle should be within reach of wheelchair-bound users. The spray pattern should be at least 0.5 m in diameter and cover both the affected individual and a helper. The emergency shower should deliver a minimum of 20 gallons of tepid water per minute. Since contaminated clothing must be removed immediately while in the shower, a modesty curtain would be an advantage. But if one is not built in, a fire blanket mounted close by might be used. Arrange with your maintenance staff to activate and check your shower monthly.

A Breath of Fresh Air

Public buildings require constant exchange of fresh air (from 5% to 15% per hour, depending upon your state's regulations). Circulation should bring air from the floor to the ceiling and then vent to the outside. Though this may increase heating and cooling bills, fresh air exchange minimizes communicable disease transfer, the growth of molds, and the accumulation of allergens in buildings. Filters and ducts on air-handling systems should be cleaned according to the manufacturer's instructions. In addition, science laboratories must have a separate air exchange system that changes the total volume of air in the room more than eight times each hour for an occupied lab and four times for an unoccupied lab, and exhausts directly to the outside rather than through the duct work for the rest of the building or into the space above hung ceilings. Because of the likelihood of chemical fumes being emitted from materials in use and in storage, the ventilation of science rooms and storage areas should *not* be controlled by energy-efficiency or timer systems that halt circulation when buildings or rooms are unoccupied. You can get great information on indoor air from the Environmental Protection Agency IAQ (indoor air quality) at 800-438-4318.

Fume hoods belong in *all* secondary science classrooms, not just chemistry labs. Chemicals used for chromatography, electrophoresis, mineral tests, and geologic and biologic specimen preservation all generate toxic fumes that belong in fume hoods. This protective equipment also belongs in teacher preparation rooms. If it is not possible to have adequate fume hoods in every science room, the curriculum must be modified or some exchange of classrooms arranged for certain lab activities. Likewise, if fume hoods are not available for every working lab group simultaneously, then the activity should be redesigned so that students participating in the fume-generating portion of the activity are conducting it in the fume hood while other students are working on other parts of the activity. Be sure wheelchair users have access to a fume hood.

When do you need a fume hood? If the label or materials safety data sheet (MSDS) for a chemical indicates it is toxic or a respiratory or mucous membrane irritant, then it should be used in the hood. Use a hood for work with materials that have a high vapor pressure or that might generate flammable or explosive vapors. In general, if the activity generates a smell, it probably requires ventilation. If regular ventilation doesn't make the smell disappear, you need a fume hood. Make sure your students know how to place their reagents and adjust the sash so the airflow is effective. Choose lab experiences that generate the fewest fumes and consider microscale work to reduce the volume of fumes produced. Consider less toxic alternatives to fume-producing toxins. And remember, the nose is not a good indicator of toxic vapors. Some chemicals, such as formalin, are above toxic levels before you can even smell them.

3

FUME HOOD FLOW

Two kinds of fume hoods are commonly found in high school science rooms—conventional appliances in which the velocity of air varies with the opening of the sliding sash and bypass hoods which redistribute air to achieve a more constant air velocity.

Many teachers mistakenly believe the stronger the current in a hood, the better. That may not necessarily be so. Most hoods should have an average face velocity (the average velocity of the air drawn through the face of the hood) of about 100 linear feet per minute. Too high a flow can cause a turbulence that can bring the vapors back into the room. Typically, the user stands at the face of the hood to work and places the reagent about 15 to 20 cm into the hood. The pull of the fans around the user's body creates eddy currents that can be strong enough to disrupt the experiment. Check the manufacturer's specifications on your hoods.

Fume hoods should be checked before each use to ensure they are in proper working order, and

- an adequate supply of outside air must be available for the hood to vent properly. Venting should go directly and completely to the outside by having the exhaust stack extend 10 to 15 feet above the roofline and an exhaust velocity of 3000 linear feet per minute.

- there should be less than 20% variation in the face velocity (for bypass hoods only). The hood should respond to changes within 3 seconds.

- hoods should be made of corrosion-resistant materials.

> drain traps for water service in the hood should be cleaned once a week by running water through them.

Proper use of fume hoods includes

> closing windows and doors during hood operation to prevent fumes from being drawn out of the hood.

> keeping the sash completely down except when inserting, manipulating, or removing materials from the hood.

> conducting work at least 15–20 cm inside the hood.

> not bypassing the fume hood or pulling reagents out for a closer look.

Seem complex? It really isn't. Some of the exercises that have been traditionally done in fume hoods probably shouldn't be done at all in a secondary classroom, while many exercises that teachers consider relatively harmless—such as chlorophyll chromatography—require fume hoods because of the solvents used. The same principles that guide your overall lesson planning should guide your use of the fume hood.

Power Up

When teachers are asked to identify the most pressing deficiencies in their classrooms, space is often the first concern, but electric service ranks a close second. As we add more electronic equipment, there never seems to be enough electrical receptacles in the right places.

Your room should have at least four separate circuits, each protected by a ground fault interrupter (GFI). These automatic devices are not a substitute for a manual shutoff or panic button. You need both. The panic button allows you to shut off power if you see a safety hazard such as a student caught in a piece of mechanical equipment. The GFI protects in cases of a short circuit.

Turn on the standard equipment you would use for basic laboratory exercises. If you are tripping circuit breakers, you don't have enough amperage to handle your needs. This often happens when you are drawing power for heating or cooling devices, such as hot plates and air conditioners. You cannot just add receptacles—you must add circuits to solve the power problem. Do not use the socket multipliers that are sold in hardware stores, because they will only increase the load on existing circuits.

There is no single ideal method of getting power to all workstations in a high school science room. But there are certainly wrong answers. Extension cords pose both fire and tripping hazards and should not be used. Loose cords should never cross aisles and pathways. If you must use a cord for a short period, cover it securely with duct tape or a shield. If workstations are located on the perimeter of the class-room, a power strip can be mounted above the counters for electric and telecommunications service.

For electric service to the middle of the room, flexibility is important. Today's perfect furniture configuration can turn into a significant instructional obstacle tomorrow. Floor outlets that project from the floor (which architects call "tombstones") pose tripping hazards and also limit the flexibility of floor plans. Spring-loaded rollers that allow cords to be pulled from the ceiling are sometimes good options, but they are tempting toys for some students and can pull lightweight equipment off the work surface, especially if the setup is jostled or shaken. Another solution is floor receptacles that are flush with the floor and watertight when not in use. Consult an architect or your school facilities supervisor for help getting the power you need—don't try to fix the situation yourself.

Telecommunications connections should be available and conveniently located close to electrical service. Consideration should be given to where different types of electronic equipment are to be located and how to make such equipment convenient to use but also protected from spills and other damaging accidents. In some cases, wireless communication has been less expensive and safer than hard-wired connections.

My Kingdom for the Right Table

A well-designed high school science room should allow a smooth flow from seat work to lab work and back again. If you have the opportunity to select your furnishings, consider flexibility and safety together—they are compatible goals. Your furniture configuration can greatly influence how and how well instruction is delivered. Sturdy flat surface worktables for two-student teams are preferable to permanently installed casework.

At the high school level, specify science-style tables with chemical-resistant tops and legs that are firmly bolted to the tabletop. Plastic laminates (e.g., Formica) are not nearly as durable as heavy resin tops. Book compartments built under student tabletops may provide convenient storage, but they also tend to accumulate trash and debris. Make sure the height of the tables matches the height of countertops where sinks are installed and that there is a station accessible to students in wheelchairs.

Tables should be light enough to be pulled up to perimeter workstations or rearranged in the middle of the room for different activities, but heavy enough to remain steady and immovable during lab work. If you are ordering tall—standing height—tables, select a style with sturdy legs and reinforcing stretcher bars near the base to stabilize the legs. Tables designed to be stable when in use but movable for rearrangement are preferred. Loose table legs are a serious hazard, so you should make it a habit to check all the tables in your room periodically and certainly after tables have been moved.

Avoid the use of stools during laboratory work. Lab activities are much safer when students are required to stand. If you have stools with backs, remove the backs to make it more difficult for students to tip back and balance on two legs. Some classrooms have lab stations without chairs on the perimeter. This may require a larger total classroom perimeter, but keeps students from being distracted by lab equipment during direct instruction and other seat-work time.

As a general rule, storage for supplies should be in fixed casework and not on movable equipment. But if you must have movable storage equipment, make sure that it is sturdy, stable, and not top-heavy when fully loaded. Wheels should lock in such a manner that the equipment will not move if accidentally pushed or bumped. The next chapter (Chapter 4, "Finders Keepers," p. 47) is devoted to the subject of storage.

Appliances such as a dishwasher, an electric stove top, a garbage disposal, and a refrigerator can also come in handy for science rooms or prep areas provided there is sufficient space and appropriate security for them. If they are present in work, storage, or preparation areas, they should not be used for preparing or storing food or cleaning utensils used for eating. If the refrigerator is used to store volatile and flammable reagents, make sure it is sparkproof and designed for laboratory use.

Special equipment and other aids needed to ensure a safe environment for special needs students may be identified in individual education plans (IEPs). The IEPs should be carefully reviewed in planning for the physical space as well as for instructional strategies.

Lights!

Lighting is a factor many teachers forget. The amount and type of lighting in your room can be a factor in student behavior and achievement. Some fluorescent lights exacerbate hyperactivity and headaches and make computer screens more difficult to read. Your classroom should have a light level of at least 50 foot-candles. A light level of 75 foot-candles is preferred for laboratory work areas. Natural light is preferable to fluorescent lighting if it can be brought in without causing glare or heating and cooling problems. Indirect lighting is better for computer screens, microscopes, and other close work. If there are cabinets above work areas, you may need lighting under them. Make sure storage areas, such as the back part of deep cabinets and corners, are also well lit.

Total room darkening is needed for many lab activities, such as optics labs, black light usage, and microprojection, so blackout shades should be specified for all science rooms. The ability to darken the area around a projector screen but keep lit the areas where students are taking notes is a definite advantage for science classrooms.

Lighting is also an important element in your emergency plan. Investigate whether all escape routes would be visible if the power fails. Building codes usually specify emergency backup lighting for halls and stairwells, but are there parts of your science classroom, prep room, and storage rooms that also require this type of lighting? Keep flashlights handy, and check batteries periodically.

Hot Stuff

Many science investigations require heat in various forms. Gas service for burners is required in most of the science disciplines but not all of the time. Each room should have a main shutoff, preferably accessible only by the teacher. We strongly recommend that the gas supply be shut off when gas is not needed.

⚡ Hot plates are often much safer sources of heat for experiments than open-flame burners. If you use hot plates, make sure they are specifically designed for lab use and are not recycled household hot plates. Check that the total amperage of all the hot plates in use at one time does not exceed the capacity of your circuits. Most hot plates have a bimetallic switch that sparks each time it makes or breaks contact. It can be a source of ignition.

Alcohol burners have been present in high school labs for generations, but they pose multiple unnecessary hazards and their use has resulted in some of the worst lab accidents reported. Do not use alcohol burners under any circumstances in high school. Unnoticed cracks can cause a burner to explode, improper filling can result in flashbacks and explosions, and alcohol supply cans are a major hazard both in use and in storage. Alcohol supply containers should never be available when students are in the room.

High school rooms may also have specialized heat sources such as drying ovens and sterilizers. We do not recommend using pressure cookers in any high school room. Autoclaves designed specifically for bacteriology should be located in secure preparatory rooms and used only by qualified staff, never by students.

Fire Protection

The most serious school emergencies involve fires. In order to meet building codes, schools are required to have features for fire prevention and fire protection. But even the best design can be defeated by thoughtless use. The keys to avoiding tragedy are prevention and preparation. It is important that teachers recognize the safety features that are part of their physical facilities and ensure that access is not blocked or obstructed.

Science rooms need two exits accessible at all times. Your classroom was probably designed to have two emergency exits. One may be a large window without a screen. Have you screened that window? Have you blocked a fire exit with furniture? The wall coverings and ceilings of your classroom should be fire resistant. Have you covered them with paper or hung combustible materials from the walls or ceilings? Make sure hanging projects and displays conform to district policy and fire codes.

You need at least one ABC fire extinguisher for your science classroom. More may be necessary depending on building codes and the size and shape of your facility. Each fire extinguisher should have a nylon or wire seal tag. Check the extinguisher monthly and notify your building administrator if the tag or seal is missing or the annual inspection is not up-to-date. Show every student where the fire extinguisher is located and make sure everyone knows how to use it. Many teachers use the mnemonic PASS to help students remember: **P**ull (the pin), **A**im (the nozzle), **S**queeze, and **S**weep (from outside to inside so the fire does not get spread). Make sure students understand that their responsibility is to notify the teacher, sound an alarm, and leave the building.

Fire Extinguishers

▶ Class A fire extinguishers contain a solution of an alkali metal salt (e.g., calcium chloride). They should be used only on fires of solid organic compounds such as wood, cloth, or paper.

▶ Class B fire extinguishers contain dry chemicals such as sodium bicarbonate. They should be used on flammable liquids such as gasoline, alcohol, flammable gases, or electrical fires.

▶ Class C fire extinguishers emit carbon dioxide. They work quickly, but when the CO_2 is gone, the fire can reignite.

▶ Class D fire extinguishers are for metal fires.

Water can extinguish only class A fires. Using water on a class B fire can make the fire worse, and carbon dioxide is a fuel for class D fires, so students should know the difference.

Make sure smoke detectors and fire alarm signals are not obscured or blocked from access. Teach your students to recognize the visual and audio fire alarm signals and respond to those signals immediately. In a science class, this means immediately stopping work, turning off equipment in the immediate work area, and evacuating. Post the fire escape route, and practice regularly. Make sure students can tell the difference between a fire alarm and the signal and procedures for windstorms or earthquakes.

Before any lab exercise that involves flame or heat, teach students how to respond if hair or clothing catches fire. Make sure they know not to run or do anything that will fan the flames, and have them practice "stop, drop, and roll." If you have a fire blanket or safety shower, teach proper use and review the use of safety equipment before every instance where this equipment might be needed. Science rooms should also have sprinkler systems that operate automatically.

See if your local firefighters are willing to do a courtesy inspection to advise you of ways to make your facilities and lab practices safer.

Many of the materials you use in the classroom will have the National Fire Protection Agency (NFPA) diamond identifying the type, potential severity, and relative fire hazard that the material might generate. The NFPA can be reached at *www.nfpa.org*.

Remember, however, that the NFPA labeling system is 50 years old and is not intended to provide information about chronic exposure. It can also underestimate the potential flammability of the material in a larger fire. It was developed to protect firefighters from the hazards of chemicals under fire-fighting conditions. But the diamond does provide some basic information to first responders when they confront unfamiliar material. It's also an easy graphic to teach, even to students with limited English proficiency, along with the standard icons for toxins, corrosives, and other hazards. (The material safety data sheets discussed in Chapter 4, p. 52, provide more accurate information on chemicals you use or store.)

Signs and Symbols

Labeling in your classroom is educational and enhances safety. Make sure your room number is clearly displayed outside and inside your room and that your students know what the room number and location are. Post the room number, location, and important emergency phone numbers and extensions at the telephone or intercom and right beside the fire, storm, and earthquake procedures. Indicate where supplies and special safety equipment are stored. In an emergency, you may be incapacitated, so students need to know how to respond without your direction.

Poison

Combustible

Biohazard

Explosive

High Voltage

Corrosive

Make signage an integral part of your room organization plan. Label where things belong and where they do not go—"no paper products in this cabinet," for instance. Use graphics and symbols as well as worded labels and instructions. Use bilingual and Braille signage as needed. Display instructions for maintenance and organism care responsibilities. Provide prominent indication of the locations of all emergency equipment, and keep the equipment accessible. Keep eye protection on display with signs describing proper use and cleaning.

Clear reagent labels are vital to safety. All chemicals (individually dispensed portions as well as stock containers) need accurate labeling. There should be no unlabeled reagents in your classroom. Labeling is not just for you and your students. It is also essential for the safety of the support staff who clean and service your facilities. For more on labeling, see Chapter 4.

Building for the Future

Be careful what you ask for—you just might get it. A renovation project may bring more safe investigations within your reach, but the process of renovation has many potential hazards and inconveniences built in. If you have contractors on site for renovations, you have special challenges for your program and for the safety of your students.

Your school's renovation project should have an on-site supervisor who is familiar with the site and can act on behalf of everyone who must continue to work in the building. Make sure the responsible contact person is aware of special considerations for maintaining safety for your science program. On-site supervisors know their job, but don't necessarily know yours.

Be conscious of ventilation patterns that might be disrupted. If your room will be temporarily less well ventilated, or if you will have less natural light, modify your program accordingly.

Make sure the construction contact person is aware of any potentially hazardous materials or equipment present in your classroom—especially those things that could be harmful to construction workers if there were a spill or other emergency.

During the renovation period, look over your plans with an eye towards simplifying and refocusing some of the activities. You are likely to find you will not be able to accomplish as much in your science program. You and your students may be more distracted, exhausted, or both as the construction project extends beyond a few weeks or a couple of months. On days when excessive noise or other disruptions are predicted, consider taking your classes outdoors for fieldwork or off site on a field trip. Above all, be flexible and maintain a sense of humor.

Consider using the construction project as an opportunity to reinforce safety concepts. Give students a tour around the work, and explain where they may not go. Ask them to report any stray tools, nails, or other construction debris. You may be able to invite the on-site supervisor, project architect, or a master tradesperson to describe the safety precautions that must be taken at the site. Call it career education. (See Chapter 11, p. 164, "Guests and Others.")

Bricks and Mortar

Facilities are the least flexible part of a school program. Although there may be long-term remodeling goals for most buildings, many teachers find their current situation is very limited. What do you do if you know your classroom doesn't meet safety and facility standards and there is no immediate relief in sight?

First, clean up and clean out. Make space by removing everything you don't need from the room. You may need to box up materials by month or season. Then take a hard look at your furnishings. Can you invest in more flexible pieces or trade with another teacher? Can you rearrange to create more space?

> ### Warning
> You must document safety problems and see to it that this information is communicated to the appropriate authorities, but this does not relieve you of responsibility. If you know an activity is unsafe and still perform it with your students, you can be held liable for purposefully and knowingly placing students in danger. Documenting a safety problem in writing is strong evidence that you know an activity is dangerous. You do not want to hear an attorney say, "So you continued to do a dangerous lab even though you knew the facility was not equipped to do it safely?" See Chapter 11, p. 167, for more information concerning liability.

Prioritize your maintenance requests, and document them. Don't fall victim to the "they won't do it anyway" attitude. Repeat your requests at regular intervals, and explain to your administrator what choices you are forced to make until you can get repairs made.

Downsize your lab experiences and your storage needs. Then remember that science is everywhere. While you wait for better facilities, use the facilities you have to expand your students' understanding of the world—and of safety.

Then let your administrator know all the positive things you have done and what you cannot do because of your concern for safety and liability.

THE SAVVY SCIENCE TEACHER

Mr. A was a veteran teacher, but he was going to be the new kid on the block in Washington High School. After signing his contract in late July, he found out that he was assigned three different preparations in two separate classrooms. In one class he had so many special needs students that a coteacher was assigned. The chemical storeroom was way down the hall. He looked at the official curriculum with dismay. This physical plant just wasn't safe for the experiences he wanted his students to have in science. A paper-and-pencil program just wouldn't do—Mr. A's conscience wouldn't allow it—but neither would crowded labs and makeshift safety equipment.

Not waiting until the opening of school, Mr. A took out some chart paper. It was time for triage. List A: the labs that could be conducted in reasonable safety in his current facilities and with his current enrollments. List B: the labs that just couldn't be considered. Then there was List C: the labs that might be made safer with minimal investments.

Mr. A got permission to clean out a chemical storage cabinet filled with papers. He inventoried reagents that were mixed in with the clutter and isolated all items that were unidentified, hazardous, or not needed for the current program. He wrote a request for professional hazardous waste removal and began a computerized database of chemicals he was retaining. He collected small containers from a pharmacy and prepared labels so he could reduce the quantities of chemicals he would have to bring into the classroom.

Then Mr. A sought out the custodian responsible for cleaning the science wing and asked for a guided tour of the facilities. On the tour, Mr. A asked a few questions and found out that filing a maintenance request on a form (which nobody else seemed to have known about) would result in the custodian's getting official instruction on how to clean the duct work and filters in Mr. A's work areas and that another form could put repair of the fume hood at the top of the maintenance list for the new school year.

Mr. A scheduled a meeting at the special education office. He and the special education supervisor brainstormed several possible remedies—redistribute the special need students so that fewer would be in any one section, schedule regular planning time for Mr. A and his non-science-trained coteacher, revise laboratory activities to accommodate the issues identified in the students'

IEPs—and arranged for Mr. A to meet the high school special education coordinator as soon she returned from summer vacation.

Then came the meeting with the principal. A new teacher with a wish list already? But Mr. A's List C became Exhibit A. When Mr. A explained what he had already accomplished and what more he could do with minimal investments, the tone of the meeting improved.

Mr. A's program won't be complete this year, since not every laboratory activity could be conducted safely. But with new allies on his professional team, he's well on the way to a safer investigative science program.

3

Connections

▶ American Society for Microbiology hand washing information. See *www.microbe.org/ washup/wash_up.asp.*

▶ ANSI Z87.1, American National Standards Institute. See *www.ansi. org* and *www1.ivenue. com/coltslaboratories/ filecabinet/ansicompar. pdf.*

▶ Biehle, J., L. Motz, and S. West. 1999. *NSTA guide to science facilities.* Arlington, VA: NSTA Press.

▶ Environmental Protection Agency IAQ INFO 800-438-4318. See *www. epa.gov.*

▶ Fume Hoods Fact Sheet, Office of Environmental Health and Safety, University of California Berkeley, 11 September 2003. *www.ehs.berkeley. edu/pubs/factsheets/ 09fumehd.html.*

▶ Laboratory Safety Institute. Designing, remodeling, and building safer labs. Natick, MA: Laboratory Safely Institute.

▶ Lowery, L., ed. 2000. Appendix C in *NSTA Pathways to the science standards—elementary school edition.* Arlington, VA: NSTA Press.

▶ MSDS (materials safety data sheet). See *www. flinnsci.com/homepage/ cindex.html esf. uvm. edu/uvmsafety/ labsafety/chemsafety/ netmsds. html msds. pdc.cornell. edu/ msdssrch.asp.*

▶ National Fire Protection Association. See *www. nfpa.org/catalog/home/ index.asp.*

(continued on p. 46)

Connections (cont.)

▶ National Institute for Occupational Safety, Chemical Safety. See *www.cdc.gov/niosh/topics/chemical-safety.*

▶ NFPA 45, Standard on Fire Protection for Laboratories Using Chemicals. See *www.nfpa.org/Codes/NFPA_Codes_and_Standards/List_of_NFPA_documents/NFPA_45.asp.*

▶ NFPA 101, Life Safety Code. See *www.nfpa.org/BuildingCode/AboutC3/NFPA101/nfpa101.asp.*

▶ NFPA 5000, Building Construction and Safety Code. See *www.nfpa.org/catalog/product.asp?pid=500003&target%5Fpid=500003&link%5Ftype=search&src=nfpa.*

▶ Occupational Safety and Health Administration. See *www.osha.gov/complinks.html.*

▶ OSHA, Hazard Communication. See *www.osha.gov/SLTC/hazardcommunications/index.html.*

▶ OSHA Regulations (Standards - 29 CFR) "Laboratory Standards" Occupational exposure to hazardous chemicals in laboratories. - 1910.1450. See *www.osha.gov/pls/oshaweb/owadisp.show_document?p_table=STANDARDS&p_id=10106.*

▶ OSHA Regulations (Standards - 29 CFR) "Chemical Hygiene Officer and Program" National Research Council Recommendations Concerning Chemical Hygiene in Laboratories (Non-Mandatory) - 1910.1450 App A. See *www.osha.gov/pls/oshaweb/owadisp. show_document?p_table=STANDARDS&p_id=10107.*

▶ Sarquis, *2000. Building student safety habits for the workplace.* Middletown, OH: Terrific Science Press.

▶ SIRI, Vermont Safety Information Resources, Inc. See *www.siri.org.*

Finders Keepers
Essentials of Safer Storage

On a fantasy island, every science teacher has an adequate budget with sufficient equipment and consumables to conduct an active program safely. On this island, teachers don't hoard things in their cabinets and storerooms, just in case. But, in real schools, teachers save what they need and what they might need tomorrow, accumulating year after year. The result is a safety hazard.

The Stuff of Science

Whether in an old building or in newly constructed quarters, there never seems to be enough storage space for the typical science teacher. It may be our insecurity over long-term budgets, or our creativity. It may be the constant time crunch that prevents us from organizing and thinking through what we put away. But we always store more than we need. It doesn't take long for the accumulated materials to overflow storage areas, take over valuable counter surfaces, and start blocking access to safety equipment, aisles, and exits. Even worse, the chemicals and materials that science teachers hoard can be downright dangerous.

Properly managing and storing all the "stuff" needed for an active science program requires both knowledge and discipline. It requires thorough knowledge of the materials and their potential for harm. It also requires teachers to plan like generals and cooperate like roommates, while maintaining a level of security the local bank would envy. Then there is the most difficult discipline of all—keeping only what is absolutely necessary.

A Place for Everything

Well-designed science rooms have cabinets that are varied and specialized—long, flat spaces for posters, tall, narrow places for graduated cylinders and microscopes, and everything in between. But science classrooms should not be the only places where the materials for laboratory work are stored. Separate, secure science storage rooms are also required. Storage and prep rooms should be situated as close to point of use as possible, preferably with direct access to the science classroom so that materials never need to be transported through the halls.

Just as science classrooms need special features, so also do storerooms: specialized storage cabinets, special air handling, and emergency equipment. Chemical storerooms should not be combined with preparation rooms. That would pose a serious hazard to the teacher. Even with extra ventilation, the air in chemical storage rooms is likely to have toxins in quantities that may not be detected but could prove harmful with prolonged exposure. If an accident occurs during preparation and you are working in a chemical storage room, the proximity of stock quantities of chemicals could be disastrous.

The prep room has a different purpose than a storeroom. Well-equipped spacious prep rooms are especially valuable if teachers do not have access to their own classrooms for preparation prior to meeting with students. These prep rooms should have emergency equipment such as showers and eyewashes as well as separately lockable storage cabinets—mobile or not—to secure materials that have been prepared. Prep rooms should not be used as offices.

Students should never be permitted to enter storage rooms. Neither should students be permitted unsupervised in the preparation room—even your most reliable, responsible students. Although you may find this impractical, the safest strategy is never to have anyone working alone in a science area, even you. In case of accident, there should be someone available to help or to summon help.

Safe and Secure

Images of mad scientists working in messy laboratories fill the media. At least a few students in any given high school will be curious about the power of the chemicals and equipment you store. So a critical element of a safe storage system is security.

All science-related rooms—classrooms, storage rooms, and preparation rooms—should have a lock system for which only the authorized teachers and specific custodial staff have keys. A keypad with a revisable code may seem better than a regular key system, but all users must be careful they are not observed while punching in the code. Probably the most secure lock system is a card-key system for which each user is issued a unique card. The time and date of each entry can be matched to individual cardholders, and cards can be rendered inoperable by the system administrator. Storage rooms and preparation rooms should each have separately locked doors with keying different from classroom keying. Their doors should be separate so that no one can enter the storage and prep rooms just by using the regular classroom key.

Storage in the Classroom

Classroom storage may be the most convenient, but consideration should be given to what is appropriate to have in the classroom and how storage units are distributed around the classroom.

Casework and Cabinets

Many science classrooms are equipped with glass-doored cabinets. Everything needed for classes and often some things not needed—chemicals, glassware, preserved specimens, and mysterious equipment—are there for all to see. But experience has shown glass doors are not good practice. They contribute nothing to security and are too easily broken. Things stored behind the glass tend to get messy and can become significant distractions to students.

In-class storage may be provided for glassware, models, and other nonconsumable lab equipment. Storage may be distributed throughout the room, occupying space on at least three of the four walls. Students can help with the distribution and storage of most equipment. Use lots of labels and organizational diagrams around the room and on classroom cabinets so everyone can see where everything is kept. You might want to use tote drawers or dish tubs to store and distribute all items needed for a particular activity or for each student work team. Include a laminated card with a list of the supplies and safety precautions. This type of system can be very convenient for lab setup and cleanup and for visual learners and absentees.

Most state and local building codes require that nonmovable cabinets be anchored to the wall so they cannot possibly cause injury in a tipping accident. Even if there is no such code in your district, check all your cabinet and storage units for proper stability and insist on having the units anchored to the wall. Movable carts may also be prone to tipping, especially tall ones such as those used for large televisions or video displays. Be sure to lock and anchor movable equipment carefully and check for stability before attempting to move it.

A Little More Security Is Better

Some useful items are too dangerous or tempting to be stored in the classroom.

Although it may be convenient to have equipment stored in the classroom, you should also consider whether security in the classroom is sufficient to protect against loss of expensive instruments. Balances, in particular, should not be left out in the classroom. They have very high "street" value—they can be used for measuring drugs—and are among the most frequently stolen items from high school laboratories. If they are so frequently used or so sensitive that it is unreasonable to store them elsewhere, then consider having them locked or bolted to permanent fixtures in the room. Give similar consideration to computer equipment, particularly laptops.

Chemical stocks should not be stored in the classroom. Transfer the amount of material needed for the activity into a properly labeled container or containers for use in the classroom. This protects the stock from contamination. (How many students remember to pour only out and never to place anything into the stock bottle?) It also reduces the potential harm should the chemical be reactive or be stolen.

If you wish to further subdivide chemicals for distribution, labeled medicine dose cups or party candy cups make good containers for dispensing small quantities of chemicals. Remember that smaller containers are still required to have the same labeling information available as for the stock bottle. Computer-generated labels can include the graphic hazard codes as well as material safety data sheet (MSDS) information that students should be taught to recognize and understand.

DESIGN YOUR OWN CLASSROOM?

If you have the privilege of designing or remodeling a science classroom, build safe storage into the walls. Include many lockable cabinets with slots for labels. Consider a one- or two-key system for all the classroom cabinets so you do not have to keep track of many individual keys. Shallow cabinets can be built behind the chalkboard or projection area, behind bulletin or chart boards, and in other spaces to maximize your ability to keep the materials you need close at hand. Shallow cabinets tend to work better than deep cabinets, because stored items can be reached more easily, and you avoid having things getting shoved back where they can never be found again. Include flat storage drawers to store posters and charts, vertical storage space for tall items such as meter sticks, and larger, low spaces for models and bulky equipment. Choose cabinets and equipment that have rounded rather than sharp corners and edges. Strong, well-reinforced wood cabinets work well while plastic laminates may be less durable. Metal cabinets tend to have sharp corners and edges and may become corroded.

Any open-shelf storage should have lips or dowel fences along the outer edge to prevent items from falling off. You should also check for seismic requirements that are part of federal, state, or local building codes.

4

Chemical Storage

Chemical storage is an issue for all science teachers, not just the chemistry instructor. The most important thing to remember is that *less is better*—less quantity, less potency, and less handling.

SCiLINKS.
THE WORLD'S A CLICK AWAY

Topic: chemical safety
Go to: *www.scilinks.org*
Code: SHL51

Material Safety Data Sheets (MSDS)

A material safety data sheet (MSDS) is a standard document available for every hazardous chemical manufactured or sold in the United States. It contains information in a specific format so users and emergency personnel can find needed information expeditiously.

Federal and many state laws require that MSDSs be available *all the time* for *every* chemical you use or store. Administrative and noninstructional staff, teachers, students, and emergency responders must have easy access to them. For practical purposes, there should be at least two sets of documents. A complete set of MSDSs for everything in the building should be kept in the main office. A set of MSDSs for items stored in a specific location should be at that location. Your local fire department should also be provided with an inventory and map of materials stored and the location of the MSDSs for the materials. First responders need to know what they might encounter in a fire or other emergency.

You may be surprised to learn that "every chemical" includes everyday items such as markers, dish and hand soaps, and even cooking items such as baking soda. When chemicals are ordered through the regular purchase order system, the requisition should specify that the vendor "Provide MSDS with order. Shipment must have MSDS to be accepted." The preferred method for meeting the MSDS requirement is to train whoever is responsible for receiving and accepting packages to look for the MSDSs before accepting the shipment. If the required MSDSs are not in the shipment, the shipment should be refused. Once the package is transferred to the intended recipient, the first thing to be done is to make copies of the MSDS and make sure that copies are filed properly in the main office master file and in each location where items are used or stored. Accepting a shipment without an MSDS and holding up payment does not accomplish the requirement of having an MSDS on file for every chemical present in the building.

When a common supply such as glue is available for teachers to take from central storage, there should be multiple copies of the MSDS available to take along with the supply. If you take supplies from the office, you need to take the MSDS along for your MSDS file. The location of MSDS files should be readily apparent in every room.

If you need to bring chemicals from home or purchase them at a convenience store because they are less expensive, you must obtain the MSDSs yourself. You can sometimes find a telephone number on the bottle. A good source of MSDS information for common household products is the Vermont SIRI site. (See "Connections" at the end of this chapter.)

MATERIAL SAFETY DATA SHEET—BLEACH LAUNDRY ORGANIC CHLORINE

(Abbreviated version)

General Information

Item Name: BLEACH LAUNDRY ORGANIC CHLORINE
Company's Name and Address: _____
Company's Emerg Ph #: _____

Ingredients/Identity Information

Proprietary: NO Signs/Symptoms Of Overexp: INHALATION: IRRITATION TO NOSE, THROAT, MOUTH SEVERE IRRITATION AND/OR BURNS. EYES: SEVERE IRRITATION AND/OR BURNS CAN OCCUR.
Emergency/First Aid Proc: EYES: FLUSH W/LG AMTS WATER—15 MIN, OCCASIONALLY LIFT UPPER/LOWER LIDS. CALL DOCTOR. SKIN: FLUSH—15 MIN. CALL DOCTOR. REMOVE CONTAM CLOTHING AND WASH BEFORE REUSE. INGEST: DON'T INDUCE VOMIT. DRINK LG AMTS WATER. DON'T GIVE ANYTHING BY MOUTH IF PERSON IS UNCONSCIOUS OR HAVING CONVULSIONS. INHALE: REMOVE TO FRESH AIR. IF BREATH HARD, GIVE OXY. KEEP WARM/REST. IF BREATH STOPS, GIVE CPR. CALL DOCTOR.

Precautions for Safe Handling and Use

Steps If Matl Released/Spill: IF SPILL IS DRY, CLEAN UP W/CLEAN, DRY DEDICATED EQUIP & PLACE IN CLEAN, DRY CNTNR. SPILL RESIDUES: DISPOSE OF AS NOTED BELOW. NEUTRALIZE MAT'L FOR DISPOSAL. CALL 1-800-654-6911
Waste Disposal Method: PRODUCT DOES NOT MEET CRITERIA OF HAZARDOUS WASTE. AS A NONHAZARDOUS SOLID WASTE, DISPOSE OF PER LOCAL, STATE, & FEDERAL REGULATIONS BY TREATMENT IN A WASTEWATER TREATMENT CENTER.

TAKE CARE TO PREVENT CONTAMINATION FROM THE USE OF THIS PRODUCT. COOL, DRY, WELL-VENT AREA. DO NOT STORE ABOVE 140 F OR IN PAPER/CARDBOARD. KEEP CLOSED & FROM MOISTURE.
Other Precautions: ADDITIONAL RESPIRATORY PROTECTION NECESSARY WHEN SMALL, DAMP SPILLS INVOLVING PRODUCT OCCUR, WHICH RELEASES CHLORINE GAS. FULL FACE CARTRIDGE-TYPE NIOSH APPROVED RESPIRATORY W/CHLORINE CARTRIDGE RECOMMENDED. USE SELF-CNTND BREATHING APPAR.Ingredient: SODIUM CHLORIDE
Ingredient Sequence Number: 01
Percent: 45-50

(cont.)

MATERIAL SAFETY DATA SHEET—BLEACH LAUNDRY ORGANIC CHLORINE

(Abbreviated version, cont.)

Proprietary: NO
Ingredient: SODIUM TRIPOLYPHOSPHATE
Ingredient Sequence Number: 02
Percent: 25-30 Proprietary: NO

Ingredient: SODIUM DICHLORO-S-TRIAZINETRIONE
Ingredient Sequence Number: 03
Percent: 24-28

Fire and Explosion Hazard Data

Extinguishing Media: USE MEDIA TO CONTROL A SURROUNDING FIRE. DO NOT USE DRY CHEMICAL EXTINGUISHERS CONTAINING AMMONIUM COMPOUNDS.
Special Fire Fighting Proc: USE WATER TO COOL CONTAINERS EXPOSED TO FIRE. SMALL FIRES—USE WATER SPRAY OR FOG. LARGE FIRES—USE HEAVY DELUGE OR FOG STREAMS.
Unusual Fire And Expl Hazrds: NONE. REQUIRED BEFORE EXTINGUISHMENT CAN BE ACCOMPLISHED. THE USE OF SELF-CONTAINED BREATHING APPARATUS IS REQUIRED IN A FIRE WHERE THIS PRODUCT IS INVOLVED.

Reactivity Data

Stability: YES
Cond To Avoid (Stability): ELEVATED TEMPERATURES (ABOVE 140 F)
Materials To Avoid: OTHER OXIDIZERS, NITROGEN CONTAINING COMPOUNDS, DRY FIRE EXTINGUISHERS CONTAINING MONO-AMMONIUM PHOSPHATE.
Hazardous Decomp Products: NITROGEN TRICHLORIDE, CHLORINE, CARBON MONOXIDE.

Health Hazard Data

Route Of Entry—Inhalation: YES
Route Of Entry—Skin: YES
Route Of Entry—Ingestion: YES
Health Haz Acute And Chronic: INHALATION OF HIGH CONCENTRATIONS CAN RESULT IN PERMANENT LUNG DAMAGE. CHRONIC INHALATION CAN ALSO CAUSE PERMANENT LUNG DAMAGE. SKIN: PROLONGED EXPOSURE MAY CAUSE DESTRUCTION OF THE DERMIS WITH IMPAIRMENT OF SIGHT TO PROPERLY REGENERATE. EYES: MAY CAUSE VISION IMPAIRMENT AND CORNEAL DAMAGE.

Organizing the Chemicals Stored

A good storeroom has the minimum of chemicals and consumables. Chemicals should be purchased in quantities that will be used up in one or two years.

Chemicals should be stored by category (rather than alphabetically) in cabinets and on shelves specially designed for the purpose.

▶ Cabinets for the storage of flammables should be made of material that can't burn. Most are made of special polymers that can delay, but not prevent, a fire. There is disagreement regarding whether a storage cabinet for flammables should be vented. Some believe it is appropriate to vent the cabinet to prevent the accumulation of fumes, but others believe venting introduces extra oxygen that may actually feed a fire. There is no federal requirement to vent these cabinets. Tightening the caps and sealing with vinyl electrician's tape is a simpler and less expensive solution.

▶ Acids and bases should be stored separately in corrosion-resistant cabinets that ideally are ventilated to the outside, above the roofline and away from air intakes. These cabinets are commonly made of wood, although some plastics work well. They should never be stacked on other cabinets. Be cautious when you purchase. Some cabinets claimed to be for storage of corrosives have been found to have metal supports, which can corrode and collapse.

▶ Potentially reactive chemicals should not be clustered together—separate, for example, acids from bases, oxidizing acids such as nitric and perchloric from organic acids such as formic and acetic. There are many potentially deadly combinations. Refer to the chart in Chapter 6, p. 86, "Bad Combos," for some examples of chemicals that can be dangerous when combined .

▶ Be alert to crystalline or filmy coatings on container or cabinet surfaces. They are usually signs of leaking containers or reactions among reagents.

▶ Be especially careful of the age of reactive and unstable chemicals.

▶ Some reactive chemicals should be stored in a container within another container or bucket in case the inner container is broken.

▶ Toxic chemicals require not only secure storage but also specific, and expensive, disposal procedures.

▶ Open shelving for more benign chemicals should be sturdy and solid, with short spans between supports. There should be lips or dowel fences along the edges to hold items in place in case of shaking or bumping. Shelves should be shallow (no more than 20 cm deep) so they are not more than two bottles deep.

▶ Avoid shelves that are placed too high. Labels are hard to read, and the bottles are more likely to tip or be dropped when reached for.

▶ Store heavier bottles on lower shelves. Be careful to consider potential reactivity if something above should fall on something stored below.

These are basic principles for the design of your chemical storeroom. But just because you now know how to store corrosive, reactive, flammable, and toxic chemicals does not mean they should be there. The science programs of 10 and 20 years ago required more and stronger chemicals than today's curricula. If your school was built then—or if you inherited materials from another building—you may have many more chemicals in your storeroom than you need. That means it's time to call a reputable hazardous waste disposal firm.

If your program requires acids, bases, or other potentially corrosive chemicals, it is better to purchase small prediluted quantities and consider alternatives to lab activities that require strong chemicals. (See Chapter 10, p. 148, for some safer alternatives.) Review all of your lab activities to see if they can be done in microscale. A microchemistry approach uses small amounts of chemicals, droppers, and clear plastic plates with test wells that reveal changes clearly and wash up quickly.

AGE DISCRIMINATION

Chemicals are not like fine wines. They do not grow better as they age. Many are reactive, unstable, or decompose to become very dangerous. Consider just a few examples:

▶ Ethers, highly volatile and flammable to begin with, can react with oxygen in air to form peroxides so unstable that just turning the cap can cause an explosion.

▶ Picric acid was once used to preserve specimens. It becomes an unstable explosive when dried out, however, and should not be used below the college level. If you should find picric acid or suspect something could be picric acid, do not touch or move it, and evacuate the area immediately. Just jarring it can cause it to explode. Call immediately for professionally trained help with removal and disposal.

> ▶ Many powdered reagents become so hard they cannot be removed from their stock bottles. Attempting to break up a chunk can break bottles, cut hands, and scatter chemicals.
>
> Date every purchase. Buy only what you need for one year, even if it's cheaper to buy in quantity. Consider the costs and hazards of disposal before you purchase. Properly dispose of all excess and outdated chemicals at the end of the year. Your curriculum might change, program needs might be different, or you might have another assignment. Share this important principle with the administration. They need to budget for new consumables and disposal each year.

Disposal and Cleanup

Disposal is complex and can be very expensive. Look up the disposal issues *before* you purchase something. If it's too hard to get rid of, don't buy it. Request that the school department establish a contract with a reputable hazardous waste disposal company to remove hazardous wastes all from locations.

Some materials that are quite innocuous in small quantities can do extensive environmental damage when they go down the drain. One example is phosphates, found in strong detergents and plant foods. Significant quantities cause eutrophication in small bodies of water, resulting in algal growth. Animal droppings from cage bedding can have the same effect. Even common salt can be a problem: Don't dump large quantities down the drain. Contact your local municipality for guidance on what can go down the drain. Then alert your students to safe disposal practices so they too can assist in protecting the environment.

Chemical Disposal

For chemicals you have now, look up the proper disposal methods or seek professional assistance. Although some materials can be diluted and put down the sink, remember that even the act of diluting some chemicals can be hazardous. Heavy metals such as cobalt, nickel, mercury, and lead should never be put into a water system or trash; neither should herbicides and pesticides. Simultaneous disposal of acids

At Your Disposal

▶ Be sure you read the MSDS when planning for proper disposal.

▶ Find out about federal, state, and local regulations.

▶ Your local fire department may be willing to take some hazardous wastes to use in training and emergency drills.

▶ If in doubt, consult with those who know about disposal, such as the school facilities manager, district science supervisor, risk manager, hazardous waste coordinator, fire chief, and the U.S. Environmental Protection Agency.

▶ Every school district or community should have a hazardous waste coordinator who is knowledgeable about federal, state, and local regulations.

4

No Dumping

You cannot dispose of unwanted chemical and biological waste by simply pouring the materials down the sink, flushing them down the toilet, or dumping them into the trash. Most of your unwanted materials can present hazards to the people who must handle them next and environmental hazards when they enter the waste stream or watershed. Some chemicals can be diluted or denatured and then discarded, but it is vital that the directions for these procedures be followed to the letter.

and bases and other combinations can cause an explosion in the pipes or traps that can cost thousands of dollars to repair.

Yours for Life

Did you know that, from the moment you purchase a chemical, your school is responsible for its disposal? Even if you turn it over to someone else, the fact is that if they stash it in the wrong place or dispose of it improperly, the chain of responsibility can bring the liability back to you and your school. There are many chemicals for which the disposal cost is many times the purchase price.

For example, the heavy metal salt ammonium dichromate was once used for model volcanoes, a demonstration now considered unsafe and bad practice. If you throw an old jar of ammonium in the regular trash and someone takes it from the trash, uses it inappropriately, and causes damage or injury, you and the school could be held liable for damages. Even if it were not stolen but rather made it into a landfill where it contaminated a water source, liability could come back to you and the school if the source of contamination could be traced. The chain of responsibility goes even further, even if you contract with a legitimate hazardous waste disposal company. If the company makes a mistake that results in contamination and as a result goes out of business, liability can rebound to the company's customers.

Are You a Toxic Waste Generator?

A complex system of environmental laws and regulations governs toxic waste disposal. Depending on the total mass of toxic waste generated, your school or district can be classified as a "large" waste generator requiring special permits and significant expenses. This waste includes not only your materials but also wastes such as the oil from the auto shop and cleaning solutions the custodians use. If the toxic chemicals are in solution, the total mass of the solution is counted. Do not stockpile your waste from year to year. Request that the district contract with a responsible hazardous waste disposal firm to remove hazardous wastes on a timely basis. At the same time, limit your acquisition and use of such material. Investigate alternatives and experiments that require smaller amounts of chemicals.

BEWARE THE GEEK BEARING GIFTS

To save yourself from liability, responsibility, and a lot of expensive and unrewarding work, never accept gifts or donations of chemicals from well-meaning parents, college or research labs, business and industry, or anyone else. You will not have the appropriate MSDS documents, and you cannot be certain of the age, purity, and prior storage conditions of chemicals that are not ordered and received directly from a reliable science supply house. You may even find that some of your "gifts" are actually hazardous wastes for which the donor did not want the responsibility of disposal. Some materials not subject to regulation when you first accept them may later be declared hazardous. The responsibility and cost for hazardous waste disposal becomes yours.

4

Biological Waste

Organic matter must be sterilized or otherwise decontaminated before it is discarded. If you grow cultures, make sure they are sterilized before disposal. Flood agar plates with chlorine bleach for a minimum of five minutes. Autoclaves are not recommended for waste disposal at the high school level because of hazards involved with their use. Kill molds with bleach or another disinfectant. Wrap terraria and animal bedding in plastic. You are responsible for the safety of everyone who handles the waste from your classroom, including custodial staff and trash collectors, as well as anyone who may use your classroom or preparation area after your activities.

Your Partner, the Custodian

Many teachers believe that once something is thrown away, it will not trouble them. Think again! You are responsible for the health and safety of your custodian and other members of the school maintenance team. Develop safe disposal rules and enforce them, for their sake.

★ Know the district policies and procedures for handling body fluids. (See "Standard (Universal) Precautions," Chapter 10, p. 142.) Make sure all adults who might come into contact with body fluids are prepared to use Standard (Universal) Precautions. Students should be given an abbreviated set of rules consistent with district and public health policy.

Don't keep preserved specimens for more than a year. Molds grow even in preservatives. If you have formaldehyde or specimens preserved in formaldehyde from years ago, you cannot simply throw these materials away or dump the fluids down the sink. They are considered hazardous wastes and must be handled as such.

preserved specimens

NATIVE AMERICAN HUMAN REMAINS

When you were hired 23 years ago, there was a box in the back room that was covered with dust and tightly sealed. Attached to the box was a note indicating its contents had been removed from the glass display case at the back of the room. At long last, curiosity prevails, and you open the box. Bones—human bones!

The explanation could be quite simple. There was a time when bones unearthed through construction or simple soil renovation projects were brought to schools for use as displays. They will most likely be of no archeological significance since their origin will have been lost. But some of these bones, including skulls, may be Native American, dating back hundreds if not thousands of years.

Native Americans are very concerned that their ancestral remains, even fragments, be handled with the greatest respect. If you believe you may have Native American ancestral remains, contact your principal first. Your local coroner or university should be able to determine if they are Native American remains. If they are determined to be Native American ancestral remains, the school or district administration should send a formal letter to the tribal chairman of the closest Native American tribe.

Should the bones be determined not to be Native American, then the local coroner's office should handle the matter. A quick and responsible reaction can resolve this issue with respect and common sense.

Equipment Disposal

Even the disposal of equipment can be problematic. You need a special container for sharps such as blades, broken glass, and metal pieces. (See Chapter 10, p. 143, for more information on sharps.) Instruments containing mercury must be handled as hazardous waste. There are also special disposal procedures for electronic equipment, smoke detectors, and dry cells.

The Itinerant Teacher

In overcrowded high schools, teachers may be assigned to different classrooms for different periods—"science on a cart." This practice is not safe. It greatly increases the chance for accidents. A rotating teacher is never sure of what may have been left out from the class before or what may linger on a desk or counter. Teachers do not have access to set up the room and the supplies properly, and so end up taking chemicals from stock bottles during class time or leaving setups in the room while other students use the space. When one teacher leaves and the other has not yet arrived, the classroom is unsupervised even though locked. Even worse, the newest, least-experienced teacher is frequently the one required to rotate through the classrooms of veteran teachers when the veteran teachers have their prep periods.

The ideal situation is to have each science teacher assigned to one science classroom and to have schedules in which similar classes, or preps, are grouped sequentially. Then chemicals are stored as close to point of use as possible. When this isn't possible, teachers and administrators should work together, take a hard look at the program, and make the modifications necessary to ensure safety. If any teacher must rotate, it should be the most experienced teacher that does so. Whatever the conditions and the schedules, safe and secure storage must be provided for science supplies and equipment—even if some of this storage is in the form of lockable portable units. Administrators must understand there is potential for liability if chemicals and specialized equipment are not properly stored and secured.

If you must change rooms during the day, ask for the strong, lockable, movable units that can travel with you. Be certain the units have locking wheels that keep them solidly in place. Bring only the minimum quantity of chemicals with you. Stock bottles should still be kept in a locked permanent storage area rather than in movable carts.

If you are an itinerant science teacher or sharing your lab space with another itinerant teacher, make sure there is an ongoing system for sharing information about chemicals storage and safety issues and a day-to-day communication system to keep each other informed about special projects. Classroom plants and animals are also at increased risk when science rooms are shared. It is important that all teachers sharing the space come to clear agreement on rules and procedures that will protect living organisms. (See Chapter 5, p. 69, for other factors to consider when choosing living things for the classroom.)

Backpacks and Outerwear

Storage problems aren't confined to teachers. Students seem to be carrying more and more things to and from school—so much that some of them need backpacks equipped with wheels. Contents of backpacks may create safety and security problems for the school community. Along with books and study supplies, backpacks, unfortunately, can contain items that can disrupt the educational process. They can also be used to carry away unauthorized items.

Even if you know what your students are carrying, all that baggage is a safety problem. Student clutter prevents easy access to safety equipment and emergency exits. Book bags and clothing can make furniture tip or block handicap accessibility.

For everyone's safety, book bags and outerwear should remain in lockers or closets rather than being brought into the classroom and shoved under desks. If lockers are inaccessible between classes, try to arrange a storage area in the room away from the main workstations. Ask students to use that area to stow materials not needed for your class.

By law, lockers are school property and can be searched for the general safety of the school, although, in most cases, items uncovered by such searches cannot be used as legal evidence. Student handbooks should notify students that searches of their lockers might be made.

You May Need a Meeting

If this section has given you a headache because you've seen your rooms described too accurately, it's time for a serious meeting with your school's administrator and your district maintenance director. Many teachers have inherited major storage and disposal problems and don't have the experience or funds to deal with them. At the meeting, concentrate on teamwork. Don't waste time and energy blaming former staff. Remember that a seemingly simple request to clean up old and excess supplies may require longer-range district planning. When budgets are tight, funds may be unavailable right away but should be reserved in the next budget round. Just plan for the future. You may need a special allocation of funds or the services of a professional environmental hazard disposal firm to make your storage facility safe again. Once you have legally disposed of old chemicals and equipment, make sure they don't accumulate again.

Be Ruthless—Be Smart

Whether you are moving into renovated or new quarters, or just returning to old ones, each year you should take a hard look at your inventory. Consider the program needs for the coming year, and keep very little else. Excellent high school programs

---

Three True Storage Stories

▶ A high school teacher accepted a sample of phosphorus from a friendly parent and kept it in the storeroom with a collection of elements. It was stolen and carried home in a student's pocket. The student's body heat caused it to ignite, resulting in severe burns.

▶ A teacher in a high school reported to police she thought some chemicals were missing, but couldn't be sure because the inventory was out of date. Investigation revealed a high school student had been gradually taking the chemicals home with the aim of making explosives.

▶ A teacher moved into a renovated classroom where she found several rusty containers of chemicals, including one with the illegible notation: "P... Acid." Fearing the container held picric acid, a school official had to call the bomb squad to remove the old bottle.

can function with limited storage, but it takes knowledge, care, and constant vigilance to do so.

Absence Makes the Lab Grow Sounder

Almost every teacher has experienced the problem: This year's budget is small, next year's may be nonexistent. You bought these washers and soda straws yourself. If you don't put them in the drawer, you may need to buy more next year. So the drawer fills up with three washers, four soda straws, two big alligator clips, a couple of dying batteries, and some spilled fish food.

Rule 1: Anything you haven't used in two years you probably don't need. And realistically, if you decide you do need it, you probably won't be able to find it and will buy it again.

Rule 2: Never accept hand-me-down chemicals and most specialized equipment from another school, generous parents, or industry. A manufacturer's reagent chemicals are usually stronger than you need. Chemicals have shelf lives, and hand-me-downs may be of uncertain age and purity. The contents may have been contaminated by use. As the new owner, you will become responsible for disposal, which can be very costly.

Rule 3: Date your purchases. (See "Age Discrimination," p. 56.) If you have access to a chemical database software program, enter each purchase. At the very least, mark the date of purchase with indelible marker on the container and in the MSDS notebook.

Rule 4: Get a good storage guide for everything you buy. Catalogs and information from science supply companies often have safe storage and handling information.

Rule 5: If you can reduce the amount of stored items, do so. Scan worksheets to disk. Keep a Web address list rather than catalogs for supplies. Almost all companies have online catalogs now.

Rule 6: Never ignore a spill or a cloudy film on the inside of a chemical-storage cabinet. They are clues that the chemicals you have stored may be reacting or decomposing, or containers may be broken or leaking. Never leave a jar with a rusted cap or crack in the cabinet. Spills and vapors are dangerous in themselves and even more so when two or more combine.

Your Second Home

Good storage and safe disposal procedures are even more important for you as an employee than for your students. Keep your second home as safe and secure as your primary residence. A stored chemical releasing a very low concentration of vapor may never be noticed by students or other temporary occupants but could trigger an allergic reaction or even worse in the classroom teacher who is in the room all day. Long-term exposure to heavy metal compounds, formaldehyde, and other items found in some science classrooms has been associated with a variety of medical problems. In a high school, you may also be responsible for shared spaces and environments. So many people may rotate through the rooms each day that extra care is needed. Many science teachers develop chronic allergies and other conditions that could be related to extended low-level exposure to environmental chemicals.

The good news? It's possible—and better practice—to do a great, hands-on high school science program with safe chemicals of low toxicity. Today's high schoolers work so hard to look sophisticated and savvy, it's easy to forget they need to explore simple phenomena. Experiences with familiar products can be memorable and are more developmentally appropriate for high school students than mysterious alchemy. It is also easier to maintain a safe, organized inventory with small amounts of less hazardous materials than to manage loaded shelves and cluttered storerooms.

THE SAVVY SCIENCE TEACHER

Great news: The science department was finally going to get some needed renovations.

Bad news: Everyone had to pack up their gear and move to portable class-rooms at the far end of the campus for the next school year.

Good news: The temporary facilities were better than the rooms that were being abandoned. Everyone would have sinks with hot and cold water, safety showers and eyewashes, and air circulation according to code. Even the storage units in the portables were better. Because all the science classrooms would be close together, the chemical and equipment storage rooms would be near everyone's classroom.

Bad news: The storage space in classrooms and storage rooms was much smaller—only a third of the combined capacity of the old building.

Tough love solution: Pitch in and pitch out. Everyone in the department had to do it.

▶   Old papers, clippings, magazines, posters, bulletins, 10-year-old science supply catalogs—some fell apart as they were lifted. File cabinets were emptied. The favorite old tests and lecture notes were scanned and saved on CD-ROM.

▶ Broken parts of anatomical models, old engine parts, wiring harnesses from a demo long since abandoned, and a couple dozen power cords were found to have no chance of repair were sent to the recycling bins along with many more unidentifiable items.

▶ A leaf and nut collection had crushed an old paper wasp nest. Old logs, branches, and bracket fungus specimens filled two supply closets. All were destined for the composter.

▶ Several bags of moldy animal bedding and a 30-gallon trash can filled with bug-infested birdseed were found in a closet at the back of the bio storeroom.

▶ Buckets contained already dissected sheep eyes, beef hearts, and fetal pigs. Because they were immersed in formaldehyde, they had to be treated as hazardous waste.

▶ At least one drawer full of worn-out batteries was found in almost every lab. Several dozen mercury-filled thermometers and weather instruments were gathered. These items also were hazardous waste.

▶ No one expected a 500-gram bottle of sodium cyanide and half-exposed sticks of yellow phosphorous—disasters waiting to happen.

▶ Then came the finds from old glass cabinets in the Earth science, physics, and bio labs: petroleum ether, carbon tetrachloride, lead solder, and concentrated nitric acid turned deep orange in color. Almost every teacher found bottles with labels so damaged it was impossible to identify the contents.

▶ An emergency contract had to be issued to a hazardous waste removal firm. They came in with chemical suits, masks, and barrels. The final bill: almost $8,000.

It took most of the first month of summer vacation to finally sort through all that had been saved. Even though the teachers were paid, it was hard work, physically and emotionally. All agreed they had been living on the edge of disaster and vowed never to let it happen again.

4

4

Connections

▶ Cornell University Environmental Health. See *www.ehs.cornell. edu.*

▶ U.S. Environmental Protection Agency is responsible for hazardous waste. See *www.epa.gov/ ebtpages/wastes.html.*

▶ Vermont Safety Information Resources, Inc. See *siri.uvm.edu/ msds.*

Lively Science

Living Organisms and More

The transformation of high school biology from a "march through phyla" to the biology and chemistry of living systems has been both exhilarating and challenging. Today's students examine ecosystems, mitochondria, and DNA, applying concepts and laboratory skills at macroscopic and microscopic levels. Courses encompass biochemistry, biophysics, biotechnology, biostatistics, and more. Today's biology teacher needs to safely manage chemicals, electronic and optical equipment, and perhaps the most complex of all—living organisms.

5

Where Have All the Flowers Gone?

At the heart of it all, biology is still the science of life. Observing and studying living organisms is critical to a good, strong program. Whether in the field or in the classroom, as a small part of a larger ecosystem or as the ecosystem with microscopic parts, the study of living organisms is at the core of the discipline. Amidst all the chemicals, new equipment, and technology, living organisms need to be maintained in a safe and educationally sound manner. This requires serious effort, so it is important to remember just why it is worth all the extra work:

▶ Properly maintaining living things should support a respect for life at all levels of complexity.

▶ Observing the movement and behavior of living organisms allows students to relate structure and function, stimulus and response.

▶ Learning how to maintain healthy living biosystems provides practical experience and adds to understanding of ecological concepts.

▶ Recognizing the requirements for keeping living things healthy can become a springboard for discussion about healthy personal choices.

▶ Asking questions about living things provides the opportunity to explore complex concepts that cross academic disciplines.

Keeping live organisms in a classroom requires not only knowledge and preparation but also the proper equipment and space. Like selecting pets, selecting classroom organisms requires a realistic appraisal of your circumstances. You must check district policy for restrictions and reporting requirements. Then ask yourself: How much space do you have? How much time can you give? How much control do you have? How will plants and animals be maintained during weekends and vacations? Does an organism require a long-term commitment, perhaps many years? Are you willing to commit to a multiyear responsibility?

Is your room shared with other teachers? Is it used by night school classes? Do some students have special needs or allergies that preclude certain types of organisms? Do the behavioral problems of any students dictate additional precautions to ensure safety? Do others visit your room during change of class?

Resist the temptation to make headlines with your classroom menagerie. Some animals, such as larger mammals and exotic species, represent serious safety challenges with relatively low educational payoff. Rescuing injured or stranded animals may seem heroic but may be both unsafe and illegal. The table on p. 69 can help you make informed choices.

YEAR-ROUND ALLERGY SEASON

For a variety of reasons, allergies and sensitivity to environmental contaminants are becoming more and more common. Adults and students alike can react to organisms and materials that had never been a problem, because sensitivity can build up from multiple exposures or because heightened sensitivity can be induced by exposure to contaminants outside the classroom. Although some sensitivities may be specifically identified in individual education plans (IEPs) and other notes in students' records, many students and their parents may not even be aware of allergies to the organisms and materials you are considering for your classroom. For this reason, avoid organisms known to create problems and be particularly alert to any signs of sensitivity—sneezes, runny noses, itches, rashes, headaches, increased illness, or absences—when you bring any new organism or material to your classroom.

Latex and peanuts present the risk of serious allergies to some individuals. Choose nonlatex gloves. Use croutons instead of peanuts for calorimetry experiments.

5

Organism	Level of Care	Potential Problems
Plants	Low: need light and water; minimal care during vacations	▶ allergenic mold on plants or in soil; use sterilized potting soil ▶ toxic plants and plant parts
Aquarium fish, protists	Low: minimal care during vacations; constant temperature needed	▶ microbial infection from unclean aquaria ▶ loss of colony due to insufficient heat or cooling during vacations
Crustacea and snails	Moderate: simple foods; minimal care during vacations	▶ bacterial contamination ▶ exotic species may endanger the environment
Insects, butterflies	Moderate: cultures can become moldy; some care necessary during vacations	▶ stings ▶ infestation of classroom or building ▶ escape or release may endanger the environment
Amphibians (tadpoles, frogs, salamanders)	Moderate: maintain reasonable temperatures	▶ microbial infection from unclean aquaria or terraria ▶ loss of colony due to insufficient heat or cooling during vacations ▶ endangered species may not be collected ▶ escape or release of non-native species may endanger the environment
Reptiles (snakes, lizards, turtles)	High: many species require live food; intolerant of cold; require tight security	▶ bites ▶ bacterial, mold, and other contamination from food and water containers ▶ sensitive to temperature change ▶ high escape and release risk
Rodents, rabbits, and other mammals	High: cannot be left unattended during vacations; require tight security	▶ allergenic dander ▶ odor and molds from droppings and bedding ▶ bites and scratches ▶ zoonotic diseases ▶ high escape and release risk

5

Biota

Take a closer look at some of the species commonly chosen for classroom culture.

Bacteria

High school students should never culture environmental bacteria in petri dish systems. Infectious *streptococci* and *staphylococci* are indigenous to the population in your classroom. Although a person with a normal immune system can withstand the challenge from small amounts of bacteria, exposure to the millions or billions of bacteria in a broken or carelessly handled culture dish can quickly overwhelm the body's immune mechanisms, resulting in serious infection and disease. You could produce a major strep or staph outbreak with disastrous results. Here are some safer suggestions for microbiologic studies:

▶ Use fresh commercial cultures of nonpathogenic bacteria for staining and microbiologic studies.

▶ For demonstrations of microbial metabolism, consider using yeast or yogurt-forming bacteria. Souring milk or vinegar formation make good lessons, which can be measured with a pH meter.

▶ Test for bacterial presence and activity without multiplying the bacteria.

▶ Over-the-counter test strips from pharmacies (e.g., urinary tract infection [UTI] test strips) detect the by-products of bacterial action rather than the bacteria itself.

▶ Test for the effects of bacterial action by using an indicator such as bromthymol blue that measures pH changes from carbon dioxide. Many bacteria release carbon dioxide as they respire.

▶ Instead of culturing soil bacteria, survey the indicators or products of microbial presence in the soil such as pH, color, and texture.

▶ Measure soil biodiversity (counting types of macroinvertebrates) as an indirect index of soil bacterial action.

▶ If you must culture environmental bacteria, use the new closed culture systems available from most science education supply houses. Don't incubate environmental samples above room temperature, because the most common pathogens thrive in the warmth.

A standard tool of bacteriology, the autoclave, can be very dangerous if not used correctly. Set up the

> ### Serratia marcescens
> Although the microbe *Serratia marcescens* was once recommended for life science activities, it has been found to be pathogenic and should not be used for school science activities.

autoclave in a preparation room, and make sure you follow all safety precautions for the equipment. Pressure cookers have been substituted for autoclaves, but pressure cookers can become bombs, releasing superheated steam, and we strongly recommend against their use.

Protists

Protists can be obtained in pure cultures or identified from water samples. In either case, it's important to emphasize hygiene. Many serious diseases can be caused by protists. When collecting water samples from the natural environment, be very careful about selecting your water source. Do not ask students to collect water samples unsupervised or on their own because of risk of drowning or infection. Potentially polluted samples, including common ditch and runoff water, require special handling. When in doubt, assume water is polluted and potentially dangerous. If unpolluted pond water is not available, substitute a hay infusion or commercially prepared sample.

SCI LINKS.
THE WORLD'S A CLICK AWAY
Topic: protista
Go to: *www.scilinks.org*
Code: SHL71A

Fungi

The kingdom Fungi includes molds, mildews, yeast, and mushrooms. Many are unwanted visitors in classrooms because of their persistence and tendency to cause allergic reactions. The reproductive spores are the most troublesome. If your curriculum calls for the observation of mold growth, keep the cultures in sealed containers when showing them. Immediately after the activity, disinfect samples with a 10% solution of household bleach and follow with proper disposal in a garbage disposal or sealed bag.

SCI LINKS.
THE WORLD'S A CLICK AWAY
Topic: Fungi
Go to: *www.scilinks.org*
Code: SHL71B

Do not let students bring wild mushrooms into the classroom; some are poisonous even to the touch, and some can provoke dangerous allergic reactions. Use grocery or commercial mushroom samples.

Yeasts make excellent subjects for life science experiments. Baker's yeast is inexpensive and available in grocery stores. It is easily cultured in a sterile molasses-water solution.

MOLDS—GUESTS THAT STAY FOREVER

Once they get established, molds and mildews are almost impossible to remove. They lurk in carpeting and mats; animal bedding and litter; germinating seeds, plants, and soils taken directly from the outside; and even artifacts in the deep dark reaches of student desks and lockers. Mold spores are easily airborne, lodging anywhere, and "blooming" years later when conditions are just right. Ridding classrooms and buildings of these persistent allergens can be very expensive.

Rather than deliberately culturing molds, engage your students in a hunt for sources of persistent molds and mildew at home and in school. Identify items for disposal before molds can grow, and arrange for the safe removal of already contaminated items.

Plants

Plants are attractive, easy to maintain, and provide valuable, timely lessons. But cautions are still needed. Some common plants or parts of plants are toxic if eaten, burned, or even touched. Beware of such common species as alamanda, oleander, hemlock, poinsettias, dieffenbachia, and holly berries. (See p. 127 for illustrations of some toxic plants.)

Be explicit. Warn your students not to taste any plants or parts of plants in your classroom, at field sites, or even in their home gardens or yards unless the plants have been specifically grown for food—and even then they should taste only the edible parts. Also warn students not to harvest endangered plants or distribute non-native species.

SCi
LINKS.
THE WORLD'S A CLICK AWAY
Topic: invertebrates
Go to: www.scilinks.org
Code: SHL72

Invertebrates

For stimulus-response and life-cycle studies, many invertebrates make excellent choices. Because invertebrate metabolism is different from ours, they are less likely to carry diseases that can spread to humans. Populations of fruit flies, mealworms, pill bugs, ants, cockroaches, hermit crabs, and dermestid beetles can be raised in jars or small terraria. *Daphnia* and brine shrimp may be barely visible to the eye, but their heartbeats can be studied under various conditions with a low-power stereo "dissecting" microscope.

Although invertebrates are small and relatively easy to care for, some are hazardous and should not be collected or cultured. Some can sting or pinch. The bites of bees, wasps, and fire ants can be very painful and, to the hypersensitive, sometimes fatal. Keep in mind that the bedding or stale food from your cages can also be a source of bacteria and mold.

Fish

Aquarium fish can be maintained safely with a few commonsense precautions. Like all classroom animals, fish should come from a reputable dealer. Resist the temptation to bring excitement into your classroom in the form of notorious species such as piranhas, large oscar fish, and live sharks—the risk and liability are not justified. Remind students to maintain good hygiene, including hand washing and appropriate disposal of filter materials.

Amphibians

The commonsense rules for care of frogs, toads, and newts are similar to those for fish. Hygiene is important. A few species of amphibians (including one large toad in the southern United States) are toxic and do not belong in classrooms. Many species are endangered, so you should not collect from natural habitats.

Reptiles

Many teachers find small reptiles are convenient classroom organisms because they provide a lot of opportunities for observation and can tolerate infrequent feedings. But even small reptiles require special attention to security and other precautions.

Many nonvenomous snakes bite, and many have secretions that can cause severe reactions in sensitive students. Small lizards and geckos are preferable to snakes, unless you have good security and the experience to make sure your students and the animals remain safe. Snakes and lizards seem to attract theft and vandalism more than many other classroom objects and have an uncanny ability to escape, so take steps to secure these animals.

Large snakes, such as boa constrictors, can also pose a strangulation hazard to smaller animals, including small humans. Iguanas are very difficult to care for and are generally not recommended. Live feeding of reptiles in front of students is prohibited in some jurisdictions.

Birds

Birds bred by legitimate breeders are generally free from diseases that are zoonotic (transmittable to humans), though every year there are a few cases reported of disease transmitted by birds brought into the country illegally. The greater danger may be to the birds than to humans. Many bird species are temperamental and easily disturbed. When subject to the noises and disturbances common to classrooms, they may become ill or self-destructive. Duck and goose droppings and unsterilized owl pellets may also carry agents infectious to humans. Buy commercial owl pellets rather than dissecting those you find in the wild.

Mammals

Resist the lure of big eyes and a furry body unless you are very sure you have a healthy, calm animal and you are ready for a lot of work. Mammals can be the most difficult and demanding of classroom organisms and also carry many diseases that can be contracted by humans.

Gerbils and white mice are the easiest mammals to maintain, but they reproduce prolifically. Rabbits, hamsters, and guinea pigs are less reliable. They scratch and bite, pass on zoonotic diseases, and shed a persistent dander to which many persons are allergic.

5

If you choose to keep mammals, you should study behavioral characteristics such as hours of activity (e.g., nocturnal, diurnal), grouping (e.g., solo, pairs, colonies), reproductive activity and frequency, and be sure you can support an animal in an environment consistent with its natural habits.

Discourage students from bringing you injured animals. This could pose dangers to you and the students. For most wild animals, a special permit is required. If students report a sick animal, rather than intervening yourself, call for expert help from the local animal control officer, the humane society, or agencies specializing in rescuing wild animals.

Aliens—Escape and Release

Every time you bring an organism into your classroom, you gain a friend for life—and a responsibility. Non-native organisms must never be released into the environment. Nor should your colleagues be exposed to contending with your freedom-loving fruit flies, mice, or reptiles.

Before you start a classroom culture, think about the end. Fowl may be returned to a farm, native plants to an old field. But do not plan to release purchased butterflies or second-generation mice into your neighborhood. They can spread disease, upset the balance in the habitat, and cause many other problems.

*SCI*LINKS.
THE WORLD'S A CLICK AWAY

Topic: viruses
Go to: *www.scilinks.org*
Code: SHL74

Exotic species are not only environmental hazards but also disease hazards. Organisms that are taken from their native environment may carry microorganisms that are indigenous and innocuous to other species in the native environment but can cause serious disease and death when they cross over to species not normally found in the native environment. Teachers should model responsibility by not maintaining exotic mammals, birds, or reptiles in the classroom.

Bacteria and other microcultures can be exotic as well. Some classic laboratory experiments involve purchased bacteria, such as the formation of Crown Galls with *agrobacterium*. This is not only illegal in some states, but a serious risk to plants in most communities if the experimental species are released into the environment—even in the trash—without incineration. Unless you have excellent training, security, and disposal facilities, the best practice is to work with native species at all times.

Students as Living Laboratories

Traditional biology labs have used students as subjects and sources of tissue and fluid samples. Biology teachers are now reconsidering these practices in light of better information about communicable diseases.

▶ We recommend you do not conduct any laboratory work that involves the use of any material that includes human body fluids. However, high school biology class can present many opportunities to discuss the transmission of infection via human body fluids (e.g., saliva, urine, blood, sera, semen), and factual scientific information can be invaluable to your students. In this area, we recommend discussion over direct investigation. Check out Chapter 10, p. 141, for more information on hepatitis, which can be transmitted when human cells and fluids are used in investigations.

▶ Do not collect, type, test, or otherwise use human blood. If your curriculum requires a blood-typing demonstration, use purchased kits with synthetic antigens. It is not just using your own or your students' blood that presents a risk. The older antigens that were sold in blood-test kits were prepared from untested blood purchased "on the street" and could present hepatitis and HIV risks.

▶ Some of the newer test strip systems (for glucose and urinary protein) use bioengineered antibodies, and can be reasonably used by students in private or at home, but urine should not be brought into the classroom.

▶ Use prepared amylase, not saliva, to hydrolyze starch.

▶ If you use straws or swabs, have a container of disinfectant or specific disposal system available at each station. Never reuse any material that has been touched by human body fluids. Have a disposal plan, and instruct students to discard contaminated items immediately in a place where the custodian will not be infected.

▶ Do not use pins or any other sharp implement for sensory nerve assays. Use coffee stirrers or hair roller picks, and properly dispose of all used items.

▶ Consider all blood and body fluids to be infectious, and refer to Chapter 10, p. 142, for a discussion of Standard Precautions. Make sure you have a specific plan for disposal of any biohazard material, and that anyone who uses your classroom knows the plan and the specific procedures necessary for disposal of these materials.

▶ Before beginning any studies that involve exercise or other means of increasing a student's heart rate, make sure you inform students and parents of the activity and receive written confirmation that they have been informed and give their permission. Check with the school nurse, individual education plans (IEPs), and other records for health problems that may preclude or require modifying the activity. Never schedule these activities during hot and humid weather, and warn students to stop immediately if they sense any discomfort.

5

Before planning any activities that involve measuring students' personal characteristics, such as height, weight, body type, or family histories, consider if one or more of your students might be embarrassed as a result. If you cannot protect those students, you must find an alternative activity.

HOUSECLEANING IN LIFE SCIENCE

A life science classroom has special cleaning requirements:

- Make sure you always have a supply of liquid soap, paper towels, and hot water for hand washing and hygiene. If you use the newer hand-cleaning gels made of quick-drying alcohol formulations, use them cautiously and keep their flammability in mind.

- Following life science activities, clean desks and counters with antibacterial soap or 10% solution of household bleach.

- Remember, stains *stain*. Use minimal quantities and determine, in advance, how to clean and neutralize spills. Keep all stains secure so students aren't tempted to use them for tattoos.

- Check the toxicity and hazards of each biological stain before using. Some are suspected of being carcinogens or teratogens. Do not use hematoxylin, methyl red, or methyl orange (carcinogens).

- Designate a disposal container for biological waste. Share your procedures with other teachers and your custodial crew.

- Using disinfectants and pesticides in school buildings is now covered by federal regulations. Be sure you know and conform to the latest rulings. In general, only trained personnel may handle these items and students must be notified in advance.

- Use heat-resistant gloves or mitts for handling hot labware.

- Have nonlatex gloves available for use in cleaning spills and stains and handling preserved specimens.

- Conjunctivitis and other infectious diseases may be spread from one user to another via contamination of safety eyewear and optical instrument eyepieces. Refer to Chapter 10, p. 146, for more information.

The Dissection Dilemma

During the past decade, dissection activities have become controversial. The activities have emphasized rote memory, and taking dissection specimens from the wild has depleted natural populations. There are safety hazards, too. Sharp instruments represent a security risk. Dissection preservatives are toxic and often allergenic. On the other hand, proponents of the dissection experience argue that students can learn a lot with carefully supervised dissections structured around inquiry questions rather than just finding and naming parts. Some states require that students who object to participating in dissection must be provided with alternative instruction that qualifies for full credit.

If you do decide to dissect, precautions are in order. Treat all preservatives and preserved specimens as toxic and hazardous. Even if you cannot smell a preservative, it may be toxic. Don't purchase any company's "secret formula" without a material safety data sheet (MSDS). Do not allow students access to stock containers containing preservative fluids. Use the lowest toxicity preservatives possible, and review the MSDS for hazards, precautions, and disposal procedure. Do not keep specimens and solutions from year to year, because molds can grow even on preserved specimens. Students must wear chemical splash and impact-resistant safety goggles, protective gloves, and an apron for dissecting. (See Chapter 10, p. 146, for more information about eye protection.) Special precautions must be taken for disposal of both the chemicals and the biological material.

Some teachers have substituted dissection of fresh grocery materials, such as chicken wings and beef hearts. There are many safety advantages with those materials. But remember that they are common sources of *E. coli* and *salmonella*. You will need to have antibacterial soap for hand washing, a disinfectant for tools and countertops, and a plan for disposal of these biological materials.

Partner with Your Support Staff

Remember your custodial staff. They will be in the room working when you and the students are gone for the day. Have you informed them of your plans to keep living organisms? Do they know what is in the room and any special considerations that may be required? Are they aware of any particularly difficult, potentially dangerous, or prone to escape organisms? Are they aware of your disposal methods and what they may encounter in the trash? Is special handling required for some waste material?

Cultivate a positive relationship with the night crew. They are a vital part of the educational team. When they are included and understand your classroom goals and responsibilities, they can more effectively support your program. An apparently simple need for adequate paper towels will no longer be a struggle. Should you forget to water a plant, they will have taken care of it, because they are included as a part of the educational team.

5

Traditionally, many students have prepared skeletons from animals they have found (often using dermestid beetles). But roadkill and fallen animals should not be brought into the school. If you prepare skeletons yourself, use domestic animals, and protect yourself with nonlatex gloves as you prebleach your specimens.

In the Supply Closet

Life science activities can involve as many toxic materials and chemicals as do chemistry activities. In new construction, life science rooms are being provided the same storage and prep rooms as chemistry rooms. If such facilities are not available at point of use (adjacent to your classroom) you should still arrange to store your stock bottles in the appropriate cabinets in a secure storeroom. (See Chapter 4.)

As our understanding of toxicity increases, we must eliminate many chemicals once commonly used. If you inherited any of the following chemicals, initiate a request to have a reliable hazardous waste disposal firm remove them. You need to get these chemicals out of your room, but you cannot dump them down the drain or in the trash:

▶ Toluene and benzene—used for embedding samples.

▶ Ethers and chloroform—used for chromatography or for anesthetizing insects.

▶ Heavy metals—such as elemental mercury or chromium compounds commonly found in stains and metallic salts.

▶ Colchicine—once used for mitosis slides.

▶ Chloroform—once commonly used for insect specimen preparation.

▶ Carbon tetrachloride—a once commonly used solvent.

▶ Hematoxylin, methyl red, methyl orange—biological stains.

▶ Benedict's solution—used for sugar testing, splashes dangerously when heated.

▶ For economic reasons, most firms still supply specimens in concentrated formaldehyde solution, but prolonged exposure to this chemical can cause cancer. Ask for a less toxic preservative. Review the MSDS for all preservatives you use.

For other reagents, refer to storage rules in Chapter 4, pp. 49-56, and recommendations in Appendix A, pp. 193–195. Make sure the storeroom is secure, and the sections for combustibles, corrosives, and organics are separate.

You may spend more money, but you are better off ordering chemicals in the strength you need rather than in more concentrated forms for later dilution. Order only what you need for one year—programs may change and chemicals may decompose or become contaminated.

Biological Chemicals

Biology rooms are often located far from the chemical storeroom and lack essentials such as fume hoods and acid traps. The dangers that biological chemicals present to our students are frequently underestimated.

But many biological chemicals are even more hazardous than those used in first year chemistry. They can be insidious, because organic chemicals that are carcinogens or teratogens may not cause immediate health effects. They may also be taken for granted because only a tiny amount would normally be used. Consider the stain hematoxylin. A professional biologist might safely use less than a milliliter of solution for an entire batch of slides and handle it without direct contact. But in a classroom, we have to assume students *might* have a significant skin or respiratory exposure to this known teratogen and that a student *might* be pregnant without our knowing. So our standards of use in the classroom must be much stricter than in professional laboratories.

Many genetic engineering and DNA lab activities use stains even more toxic than those used in standard beginning biology lessons. Because these laboratories are often restricted to advanced students, the stains can be better controlled than they would be in a first course. However, biological storerooms are often farther from point of use, and you may not be aware of a pregnant colleague or student who could be exposed, so be very cautious with known teratogens. Opt for less toxic nuclear stains such as methylene blue over more dangerous ethidium bromide or toluidine blue. Also be especially careful with highly purified ethanol, which might be considered a tempting item for theft and is highly flammable.

Formaldehyde

Formaldehyde solution—also called formalin—has been replaced largely by newer, less odorous, and less toxic preservatives with a variety of trade names. However, most of these new formulations still contain formaldehyde, albeit in lesser concentrations and mixed with other ingredients meant to reduce odor and be less irritating. You should treat all specimen preservatives as though they contain formaldehyde, particularly if you or your students are sensitive to materials of this type. The *Flinn Scientific Catalog/Reference Manual* and *Safety in School Science Laboratories* contain good discussions of the issue.

5

Don't take anything for granted with chemicals. Research the most recent MSDS information for every chemical you use, and employ appropriate disposal procedures for anything that is questionable in your storeroom. See Appendix A, pp. 193–195, for information on chemicals we recommend not using.

A TASTE FOR NEW BIOLOGY LESSONS?

For decades, biology teachers have had students construct pedigrees with the "taster" gene. All it required was a supply of small strips of paper coated with phenothiocarbamide (PTC or 1-phenyl-2-thiorea, $C_6N_5NHCSNH_2$). It was quick, inexpensive, and seemed to work. But it was also inaccurate, dangerous, and downright bad science. It's time to properly dispose of the PTC paper and develop a taste for new experiences and new ideas in genetics.

PTC is one of a group of chemicals that some people seem to be able to taste more than others. Most textbooks have called the ability to taste "Mendelian" since nontasters seem to have only nontasting offspring, but it's really incomplete dominance. Tallying "tasters" leads to serious misconceptions since it confuses the genetics of PTC with its population biology. Researchers now understand that the "taster" trait isn't as simple a biochemical process as the textbooks suggest; it's a function of anatomy. Surrounding each taste bud are receptors for pain (e.g., for jalepeños) and touch sensors for fats, which are agonistic to taste receptors.. There are no special areas of the tongue for sweet, sour, salty, or bitter.

After all this misinformation, if you still have a taste for using PTC strips, here's something to spoil your appetite. PTC is sold as a rat poison. Its MSDS says it's "fatal if swallowed ... a respiratory tract irritant." If you are thinking, "That would take a lot of PTC," think again. The LD_{50} is 3.4 mg/kg. A single strip has about 0.3 mg, so a small tube of 50 strips can kill a newborn infant or a family pet. And remember, that's an average. A stolen supply of PTC strips could cause serious harm. PTC does not belong in a classroom, and especially not at a family reunion to create a pedigree. (Find out more at *physchem.ox.ac.uk/MSDS/PH/1-phenyl-2-thiourea.html*.) Substitute an herb like cilantro, or instead trace what members of your family like broccoli.

What You Don't Know . . .

Nationally, the majority of high school life science *sections* are still taught by non-biology majors. As you can see from the preceding text, biology is changing quickly. Standard laboratory exercises and materials used in bio labs less than a decade ago may now be considered hazardous and unsafe. If your training is not thorough and current, you may be teaching biology as it was taught to you in high school. Work with your administrative scheduling team to obtain the professional development you need to conduct safe science. The old-fashioned biology room with an outdated curriculum poses serious risks for the unprepared.

THE SAVVY SCIENCE TEACHER

Ms. P loves potatoes—French fries, hash browns, and the bags of Idahos that she brings to her biology class.

Ms. P used to teach her students about cell size using phenolphthalein agar. Now she uses potato cubes in Lugol's solution. Even though students must be cautious about the iodine solution, the risks are lower than with phenolphthalein.

Now liver—that's a food Ms. P always hated. So she was thrilled to substitute potatoes for raw liver in her lesson on catalase. The potatoes don't carry as many bacteria, or the potential for infection.

Potato cells have great starch bodies, and provide starch to study amylase. The buds can be saved for a lesson on vegetative reproduction. Ms. P knows that there are many other ideas she hasn't even thought of. So when school is over, she grabs a supersized order of fries and gets creative.

5

Connections

- American Society for Microbiology. See *www.microbe.org.*
- *Flinn Scientific Catalog/Reference Manual.* 2002. Batavia, IL: Flinn Scientific, Inc. See *www.flinnsci.com*
- Laboratory Safety Institute. 1995. *Safety in school science laboratories.* Natick, MA: Laboratory Safety Institute.
- PTC Tasting physchem. See *ox.ac.uk/MSDS/PH/1-phenyl-2-thiourea.html.*

Modern Alchemy
Safer Teaching with Chemistry

> *The tea turns golden as the lemon is added. Soda gets sweeter as it sits out. Concrete hardens quickly in the hot summer sun. A chocolate cake rises in the oven. Chemistry is everywhere. But so are chemical hazards—lawn pesticides, bathroom cleaners, radon gas in basements. Modern chemistry can be taught with examples that introduce students to safe interaction with chemicals in everyday living.*

Chemistry for All Students

Chemistry courses were once taken almost exclusively by college-bound students. Today we hope that all students learn the principles of matter and energy—students with diverse goals, abilities, and behaviors. We welcome in chemistry classes many more students who are not college-bound. Our curricula have been modified to include many more real-world applications—practical and motivating for all students. We also need to modify safety instruction to appropriately address the wide range of student interests and abilities, and to provide all students with ways to apply safety principles in everyday activities.

Our chemistry programs may be riddled with misconceptions, not just among the students, but the teachers. We often overestimate our students' backgrounds and may misunderstand the way they see the world. We work at dramatic demonstrations and plan lessons that move along like MTV, while students struggle with the simplest concepts and common natural phenomena. We assume they see what we see, but their perceptions are often quite different. One of the most dangerous misconceptions a chemistry teacher can have is that it takes an explosive demonstration to motivate students.

Actually, chemistry teachers may have to take some time to retrain their students to observe more carefully and for longer periods of time than they are used to. Having grown up with fast-paced media presentations, students and adults alike have come to have shorter and shorter attention spans and expect loud, flashy events to catch their attention. But real phenomena may be far subtler. Students don't need explosions; they need to be taught to look more carefully, mix more slowly, and be more aware of the hazards in their world. They need quiet think time to review what they have observed

6

and analyze their own preconceptions. The excitement of an explosion often prevents them from analyzing their preconceptions. Startle your students and gain their attention with discrepant events rather than noisy dangerous ones.

Using authentic experiences and relevant real-world demonstrations may present some special challenges for teachers. Much of the material you need may come from retail stores, which do not supply material safety data sheets (MSDS). However, you can usually find MSDSs on the Internet. (For a detailed explanation of these documents, see Chapter 4, p. 52.) Another challenge is to ensure that students take seriously the warning: "Don't try this at home." Discussion rather than simple exhortation is more likely to be effective. Don't stop with a tour of classroom safety equipment. Embed relevant safety discussion and instruction in every lesson.

Small and Less Are Better

Even when you are using familiar substances, accidents can occur. In the most disciplined room, the urge to sneak a taste of something or snatch a bit of chemical to try at home may be overwhelming. Using the smallest possible quantity of a reagent reduces the magnitude of harm the chemicals can cause. Think drops rather than test tubes or beakers full. With solids, think in granules and pea-sized proportions.

Many excellent microscale chemistry activities have been developed for the high school level. Observing a phenomenon on a small scale requires students to pay close attention to small changes and focus on detail. Set students up to discover the excitement of seeing a hypothesis confirmed, rather than seeing an experiment self-destruct.

Microscale experiments appear in many textbooks and on the Internet. At a minimum, you need two types of equipment: microchemistry test (well) plates and disposable Pasteur pipettes. The well plates come in several forms. Those with larger wells are easier to display on an overhead or with a video cam, but are harder to clean up. Guard against contamination in test plates, because they cannot be rinsed as effectively as traditional glassware. To minimize the chance of contamination, it's a good idea to keep a separate set of test plates for each type of experiment.

We've heard many teachers say: "Microscale doesn't work because my students don't notice what I want them to see." We offer two responses: First, observation is a skill, and teaching students to observe well may need to precede other lessons. Second, it's possible that what students need to see and what you think they need to see

6

may be quite different. Listen carefully to identify misconceptions when students do microchemistry.

In instances when microchemistry isn't practical, you can still scale down the quantities you use to reduce hazards. Have your students ever mixed too much sulfur with iron to form iron sulfide? By keeping the stock supply of materials such as sulfur out of the classroom and the quantity at each lab station very small, the consequences of human error can be minimized.

Behind the Shield

Many safety guides admonish teachers to put up a safety shield to protect students when performing hazardous demonstrations. But where is the teacher in this exhibition? Behind the shield! This guide takes a different approach. Today's students have seen plenty of explosions and burning rivers. But unlike their parents, they probably have rarely watched sidewalks harden, developed photos, or invented their own recipes. Select demonstrations that encourage students' concentration rather than shock and awe. Select activities that are developmentally appropriate. Focus students' attention on phenomena they may misunderstand or may never have noticed. Last but not least, make sure demonstrations are as safe for you as they are for your students.

Corral Your Stock

The stock supply of any chemical, even those you think are harmless, should always remain in a locked cabinet or storeroom. This is especially important with hazardous items such as corrosives, reactives, flammables, and toxics. Some of the most serious school accidents have occurred when the stock supply of a flammable such as alcohol was placed near a heat source. Before class, measure the quantities you need and make sure all samples are labeled. Clean plastic trays or storage tubs are handy for transporting these supplies.

The idea that the stockroom should be as close as possible to point of use is a relatively new one to architects. It's doubly difficult in schools designed for "houses," where one chemistry room is sited in each wing. If you are working in an older school or a school structured in houses, you may need to request physical modifications to make secure chemical storage close enough to your work area. Never send a student to a storeroom to obtain supplies. Do not allow students to enter storerooms or to work unsupervised in teacher preparation areas.

> ### Student Assistants
>
> Many teachers train students as assistants. If you do so, make sure you emphasize safety training and do not allow students to work unsupervised. Even the best-trained students should never be permitted in chemical storage rooms and should not be allowed to work in preparation rooms unless you are present.

6

Bad Combos

This chart represents just a few hazardous combinations of chemicals. Combining chemicals in list A with chemicals on the same line in list B can cause violent reactions or create highly toxic gases.

A	B
acids	azides, cyanides, nitrites, sulfides
alcohols (methyl and ethyl)	sodium peroxide
ammonium salts	bromine, iodine, sodium nitrate, silver
copper	hydrogen peroxide
hydrogen sulfide	nitric acid
nitric acid	acetone
permanganates	acetic acid
potassium salts	sulfuric acid
sulfuric acid	acetone, nitrates
water	alkaline earth metals, calcium oxide

There are many others. To avoid adverse reactions, store incompatible chemicals separately and in appropriate containers. Store acids and bases separately. Be alert to films on glass bottles, windows, or the insides of cabinets. They are usually signs of leaks or fumes from chemical containers. Cracked or corroded caps and containers must be replaced immediately. In many cases, breached containers may result in contaminated contents that must not be used.

Chemicals cannot simply be thrown away. Disposal is a major issue in high school science. Many materials cost far more to get rid of than to purchase. Hazardous waste disposal is governed by U.S. Environmental Protection Agency Resource Conservation and Recovery Act requirements and should only be conducted in conjunction with reputable, licensed firms. Check out their fees—it will make microchemistry all the more appealing. (Refer to Chapter 4, p. 47 , and Appendix A for more information on chemical storage and hazardous waste disposal.)

No Wiggle Room

Bumping and jostling are frequent causes of spills and accidents during chemistry activities. A way to minimize these risks is to provide as much clear work space as possible. This means you should ask students to leave all but the essentials in their lockers when they come to class. Tell them in advance when specific items such as texts are needed and ask that no extra books and materials be brought to lab classes. If lockers are too far away for students to access them between classes, arrange a storage area in some part of your room away from work surfaces for backpacks and other paraphernalia to be deposited during lab activities. Explain how sudden or extraneous motion can be especially dangerous during chemistry activities.

In general, it is better for students to stand while doing chemistry experiments to avoid the possibility of spills onto laps. Get chairs and stools out of the way so student have room to step back or make a quick exit. Sitting should be permitted only for physically disabled students and then only at benches designed for handicapped access.

Tools of the Trade

In keeping with the idea that simpler and smaller are better, look over your inventory of science equipment. Some of what you own may be more hazardous and less useful than their newer counterparts.

Mercury-Filled Instruments: If you still have barometers, thermometers, or other measuring instruments made with mercury (the column is silver in color), you need to arrange for safe disposal immediately. The danger posed by spilled mercury from broken instruments is serious and unacceptable. These instruments all have electronic counterparts that are more precise and no longer prohibitively expensive.

Instruments for Measuring Mass: Keep a few double-pan or triple-beam balances to help students learn and understand the concept of mass. But once the idea is well established, you will find that using electronic balances reduces the time required to take measurements and can produce more precise data. Lock up your balances when you are not using them. If you plan to leave them on counters or desktops when a room is not

Oldies but Not Goodies

Many of the chemistry demonstrations and materials found in old science methods books are now known to be hazardous. Refer to Appendix A, p. 193, for a partial list of chemicals that do not belong in a high school program. Review all your old favorites by checking the MSDS and a good, current website reference to see if other items should be abandoned as well. You may find that you need to request hazardous waste removal to get rid of your predecessors' leftovers.

6

supervised, bolt or chain them to the work surface. Because of their value in illicit drug activity, balances are among the most commonly stolen items from science facilities.

General-Use Containers and Instruments to Measure Volume (e.g., beakers and graduated cylinders): Many teachers are opting for plastic when glass is not absolutely necessary. Clear plastic polycarbonate containers are quite rugged and heat resistant but are also the most expensive. Polypropylene containers are translucent, making it difficult to see the liquid, and may crack more easily but are generally less expensive. Check for descriptions and suggested uses for the different types of plastics in supply catalogs. Some of the plastics are heat resistant and will not melt or deform even with boiling water, but none are flameproof, so you cannot use them with burners or stovetops. When glass is needed, be sure you order borosilicate glass that is heat resistant and flameproof. Keep movable parts such as the stopcocks of burettes clean and lubricated, and do not depend on students for the final cleaning of this type of equipment.

Even glassware that looks safe can fracture, so it is always necessary to tape glass when it will be under pressure. Everyone must wear appropriate eye protection throughout the experiment. Microchemistry is highly recommended for these activities.

Sharp Instruments: The use of cutting tools such as utility knives or scalpels and glass instruments requires eye protection. You must have disposal containers for sharps to protect personnel who handle the trash. (See Chapter 10, p. 143, for additional discussion on sharps.)

Tubing and Connectors: Substitute plastic tubing for glass tubing whenever possible. If you use glass tubing, make sure it is all fire-polished.

Students should not cut, bend, or fire-polish glass, or insert glass tubing into corks or stoppers. Even you, as an adult, should not attempt these activities unless you have had specific training to do so. Exercise extreme care and caution if you engage in this work. Cutting and inserting glass involve serious risks from breaking glass and can cause permanent injury to hands and eyes. Bending or fire-polishing glass adds the danger of serious burns, especially when hot glass does not look hot. Wear impact-resistant safety glasses. Use heat-resistant mats when you set down hot glass, and always protect your hands with something like a thick towel if you insert glass tubing. There are some tools that assist with glass tube insertion, but use them with careful attention. If your supplies are very old, you might find an asbestos mat. Turn it over to a certified asbestos remover.

Spark Generators: These should be checked before use and secured after each lab.

Electrophoresis Apparatus: Watch the voltage. (See Chapter 5, p. 78, for information on toxicity of standard stains.)

Spectrometers and Other Electric and Electronic Equipment: Check integrity of wiring and keep equipment away from water. All receptacles should be GFI (ground fault interrupter)-protected.

Calorimeters and Gas Generators: Make sure they have properly functioning pressure releases.

Heat Sources: Bunsen burners are standard for some high school chemistry experiments but may not be needed as often as they are used. Your gas supply should have an emergency shutoff accessible for use in an emergency *and* a locked shutoff for times when the burners are not needed. Gas should not be available to students at times when they are not specifically required to use it. Personally check all burners before use. If your experiment will work with slow, steady heat, consider lab-grade hot plates instead, but be cautious of heat retention after hot plates have been turned off. Never use alcohol burners. (See Chapter 3, p. 39, for additional explanation.)

Gas Cylinders: Once familiar pieces of science equipment, compressed gas cylinders are used less frequently these days. They are potentially dangerous. Don't store compressed oxygen or hydrogen under any circumstances. If there is a valid reason to have compressed air or carbon dioxide in your room, you should observe the following precautions:

▶ Obtain and refill your cylinders through licensed, reputable dealers.

▶ Examine valves and handle them carefully. Don't lift the cylinder by the valve, and make sure the valve is closed firmly when not in use.

▶ Keep the labels intact and clear.

▶ Store cylinders in an upright position secured with a chain or clamp.

▶ Store cylinders in a cool place, never near heat.

▶ Protect cylinders from bumping and tipping.

▶ Keep the protective can in place except when the cylinder is use.

Gear Up for Safety

Although many high schools debate the legality of general dress codes, in the chemistry room there's no debate. Safety takes precedence. When you insist that students dress appropriately for lab activities, you

Chemistry Students Dress for Success

▶ Use chemical splash safety goggles throughout every lab.

▶ Fasten hair securely behind the shoulders.

▶ Do not wear loose-fitting sleeves or overhanging clothing.

▶ Use lab aprons and rubber bands to hold back dangling items.

▶ Do not wear platform shoes or dragging pant legs.

▶ Remove or tape over dangling jewelry.

▶ Use appropriate gloves where needed.

6

reinforce the significance of the laboratory work and encourage students to act like science professionals.

Rather than simply banning certain types of clothing, it may be useful to involve students in assessing the hazards. Have students design and perform safety tests for various fabrics, hair gels, and accessories to help establish not just the rules but reasons for the rules. Students can contribute by identifying the latest "hot" items, because fads come and go rapidly. For example, a few years ago a type of soft, flared skirt was all the rage with teenage girls. Only after a series of tragic accidents did manufacturers and consumers realize how highly flammable they were.

Safety Eyewear: Almost every chemistry experiment requires safety eyewear. In addition to the potential for chemicals entering the eyes, you must protect against the possibility of projectiles resulting from a dropped or shattered container and materials sent flying by an unanticipated release of pressure. If there is any doubt, have everyone put on safety goggles—this includes all room occupants. See Chapter 10, p. 146, "All Eyes on Science," for a detailed explanation of eye protection.

Safety eyewear must be sanitized between uses. This can be done by hanging it in a sanitizer equipped with ultraviolet (UV) lights. But, if the next class must reuse the eyewear immediately, there may not be enough time for disinfection. Goggles piled haphazardly into UV sterilization cabinets might not get sanitized at all. A simpler procedure is for departing students to drop their goggles into a sink filled with antibacterial dishwashing solution. Entering students can thoroughly rinse and dry the goggles and wear them immediately afterward. If you use this method, make sure straps are plastic rather than cloth. Have plenty of soft clean towels available, because rough paper towels can scratch the plastic lenses. Another alternative is to have a personal pair of safety goggles for each student and instructor with just a few extra pairs available for use by visitors.

Face Shields: If an experiment requires a face shield, it probably shouldn't be done. However, you may need to use a face shield, in addition to your safety glasses or chemical splash glasses to protect the rest of your face and throat when you prepare materials away from the presence of students. This would be appropriate when diluting concentrated acids, though we recommend purchasing pre-diluted solutions. If the experiment is *absolutely* required in the curriculum, use microscale quantities and a video cam to minimize risk.

Aprons: A waterproof lab apron should be used whenever there is a possibility of spills, splash, or flame. When in use, the apron ties should be securely fastened. Worn correctly, the apron can also be used to hold back loose-fitting clothing that poses hazards from knocking something over or catching on fire. Loose-fitting sleeves should be rolled up, fastened with rubber bands, or both. Avoid latex aprons and gloves due to the possibility of severe allergic reaction in sensitive individuals.

Gloves: Use heat-resistant gloves or mitts for handling hot labware. Have nonlatex gloves available for use in cleaning spills and stains.

Tongs: Tongs are important tools for instructor use in handling hot labware, but students are usually less adept at managing them and spills often occur. You can avoid having students use tongs by preparing materials ahead of time or, in heating experiments, heat materials gently, and let them cool before handling. Heat-resistant gloves or mitts may be an alternative, but these too may be difficult to use.

When Neighborliness Isn't a Virtue

In many schools, some hazardous chemicals used in the art room are stored by the chemistry teacher. There are several dangers in doing this. Transport of chemicals for any distance through corridors is risky. Many art teachers don't have the background in chemical safety the science teacher has, and the art room may lack appropriate safety equipment or protective eyewear and aprons. In these cases, the chemistry teacher might be held liable for providing dangerous materials to an unsecured location. If you must supply or store acids (for jewelry) or glazes (for pottery) for the art program, make sure that appropriate safety equipment and MSDSs are available in both your science storage room and in the art room. Many glazes used only a few years ago are now banned because they are carcinogenic. Don't be talked into keeping those under any circumstances. Arrange for smaller, properly labeled containers for transport of materials.

Restrict Glaze Material

Glaze materials with these compounds should not be used in high school art rooms:

- arsenic compounds
- beryllium compounds
- cadmium compounds
- lead compounds
- nickel compounds
- selenium compounds
- uranium compounds
- zinc compounds

These chemicals are especially toxic when they are heated in kilns. All kilns should be vented to the outside.

6

WHAT IF...

Inevitable questions that emerge from chemistry activities are "What happens when you mix ...?" and "Will ... explode?"

Your reply should make clear it is never acceptable to mix chemicals together randomly (see chart in this chapter on p. 86). Even minute amounts of some chemicals can result in deadly combinations. Experiments should be the culmination of a careful thought process that predicts results based on extensive preparation and review of data and known characteristics of materials. Steer students to the fascination and excitement of confirming predictions and recognizing discrepant events. As Louis Pasteur said, "Chance favors the prepared mind."

Do not keep in your storeroom reagents such as ammonium nitrate, which can be used to make explosives. Let students know you do not have such materials. If you identify a student with an unusual or inappropriate interest in chemicals, don't hesitate to make a counseling referral.

Dangerous Living through Chemistry

The toxic effect of a chemical is a relative rather than an absolute characteristic. Commonly available household chemicals can be lethal to humans, pets, plants, and the environment depending on the use to which they are put, the concentration of the material, and the means of exposure. Many everyday household chemicals such as rubbing alcohol, bleach, detergents, and other cleaning agents can be toxic and dangerous when mishandled. When you think of the toxicity of a product, consider the quantity provided to the entire lab group rather than the amount a single student needs, since a container could go missing. Don't use (or even order) chemicals in higher concentration than necessary.

Exposure by absorption through the mucous membranes may be far greater than by touching. Since chronic exposure is a greater danger for you than for your students, make sure your preparation room has all the ventilation and safety equipment you would demand in your classroom.

Poison Control

American Association of Poison Control Center national hotline: 800 222-1222

Although adolescents are notoriously suspicious of advice from adults, you have the opportunity to arm your students with data and evidence rather than just an adult opinion. You can use class chemistry activities to give students firsthand evidence of hazards they may otherwise ignore. Activities that combine chemistry and biology provide excellent opportunities to discuss real-world consequences of incorrectly using and handling chemicals and drugs.

6

GUIDELINES FOR HANDLING TOXIC CHEMICALS

Many chemicals that might be appropriate at a college level are inappropriate at a high school level. When considering whether a chemical is toxic, consider the worst-case scenario—that a student is exposed to *all* of the group's allocation. Take special note of the toxicity (LD_{50}) of chemical reagents such as dyes and stains. Consider these general guidelines:

▶ Label *every* container (including the small ones for group work) with the name of the chemical, its symbol, and the word "toxic," and a description of the hazard in plain English, such as "can cause cancer."

▶ Post a warning when these chemicals are used in the classroom.

▶ Provide nonlatex gloves for handling and cleanup.

▶ Protect surfaces from contamination by using trays or pans that can be decontaminated.

▶ Dispose of materials in an appropriate manner.

▶ Decontaminate the room immediately after use.

Remember that different classes use the same room. Also remember that pregnant individuals may be at additional risk. Always minimize the use of toxic materials.

6

Sample Toxicity Levels of Common Chemicals

Chemical	Animal LD50*	150 lb Adult	Effect
Mercuric chloride	1 mg/kg**	‹7 drops	extremely toxic
Potassium cyanide	50 mg/kg	‹1 tsp	highly toxic
Formaldehyde	500 mg/kg	‹1 ounce	moderately toxic
Aspirin	5 g/kg	›1 ounce	slightly toxic
Glycerin	›5 g/kg	›1 pint	nontoxic

*lethal dose 50 (LD_{50}), the dose that results in the death of 50% of test animals

**dose in milligrams per kilogram of the animal's body mass

Source: Toxicities adapted from Flinn Scientific Catalog (2003).

The (Not So) Sweet Smell of Success

Remember the old saying, "If it moves, it's biology; if it smells, it's chemistry"? It's probably inevitable that some of your chemistry activities generate unpleasant odors. Odors are a signal that chemicals are in the air. Some chemicals have short- or long-term toxic effects while others can provoke asthma or other severe allergic responses. Be sure you fully understand the nature and toxicity of the chemical that is causing the odor, and do not generate fumes at concentrations that are harmful. Even when fumes have low toxicity, minimize odors by using small quantities.

In closed or crowded conditions, even slight odors can become major problems, because odors tend to excite students and may cause them to be less cautious. If the room you are using for lab work was converted from a regular classroom, it may not be as well ventilated as a properly constructed science room. A properly ventilated science lab has fans or HVAC systems that can exchange the entire volume of room air a minimum of eight times each hour. If your room does not meet this standard, you need to make sure strong odors and fumes are not generated. (Additional information on fume hoods and room ventilation systems is in Chapter 3, p. 34.)

Plan to conduct labs that generate odor, such as decomposition experiments, on days when the windows can be opened. Teach students the proper way to test for an odor.

THE SAVVY SCIENCE TEACHER

Dr. G has been teaching chemistry for 20 years, and every year is as challenging as the first. There was a time when she had only high-performing students. But she has recruited many other students in recent years. She has also become a consultant to the committee developing the new freshman physical science program, which will include some serious chemistry for younger learners.

Different students mean different labs. There are no more bottles labeled "unknown" in Dr. G's lab. Today there are bottles labeled "a" through "d," and four MSDSs available to each student. Students learn quickly that they must treat all four unknowns as if each were the most toxic, corrosive, reactive, or flammable and that identification information is always available to them in an emergency.

6

Reagent bottles are smaller these days; so are the test tubes and well plates. Dr. G's students have learned they have to observe carefully and record accurately to find the answers to her laboratory questions. They learn proper disposal methods along with other chemistry lessons.

With all these changes, Dr. G's students have become environmental chemistry experts. They've developed brochures for the community, which instruct on safe handling and proper disposal of household chemicals.

Connections

Good sources for MSDS information

▶ Vermont Safety Information Resources, Inc. *hazard.com.*

▶ Fisher Scientific. *www.fishersci.com.*

▶ Cornell University. See *msds.pdc.cornell.edu/ msdssrch.asp.*

Ideas for Microscale Chemistry

▶ Microscale Gas Chemistry. See *mattson.creigh-ton.edu/ThreeEasy Gases.html.*

▶ National Microscale Chemistry Center. See *www.microscale.org/ about.asp.*

▶ Samples of Chemistry Accidents. SafeChem. *See www.safechem.com/ Campusafe/accident.htm.*

▶ American Chemical Society and ACS Board-Council Committee on Chemical Safety. 2001. *Chemical safety for teachers and their supervisors.* Washington, DC: ACS. See *membership. acs.org/c/ccs/pubs/ chemical_ safety_manual. pdf.*

▶ Laboratory Safety Institute. James A Kaufman, President. *www.labsafety.org/ about.htm.*

6

Striking Gold
Exploring Earth and Space Sciences

Earth and space sciences—the final frontiers. Spurred on by tales of adventure, most students are enthusiastic explorers. But, as astronauts, oceanographers, and geologists know, these frontiers have their dangers for which explorers must be prepared. From wearing protective clothing and equipment to using proper techniques with tools, there is much to learn. Above all, remember there's gold in down-to-earth common sense.

Earth-Shaking Sciences

Modern Earth and space sciences are multidisciplinary and incorporate many of the concepts in life and physical sciences. In many states, this course has traditionally been an elective or a general introductory course. Recognizing the complexity of the concepts, the national trend is to move this integrated science to the junior or senior year. Whether the course is at an introductory or freshman level or a capstone course, it will challenge students to demonstrate safety precautions relevant to other courses. These skills and habits combine common sense with scientific knowledge and may be best remembered when you show students how safe practice applies equally to situations in students' daily lives.

An Earth and Space Science Room Is Anywhere You Find It

When there are fewer science rooms than teachers, it is often Earth science teachers who find themselves moving from one science room to another, filling in during others' free periods, or worse yet, trying to teach in a regular classroom rather than a lab classroom. Finding the proper facilities for the course will be especially challenging to teachers building new curricula in older schools.

7

Because of its multidisciplinary nature, Earth and space science requires most of the facilities and safety features of physics, chemistry, and modern biology rooms. (Refer to Chapter 3, p. 27, for more information.) If your course must be fit into an existing facility, here are a few features you should try to incorporate:

▶ *Furniture, such as work tables and storage shelves, strong and stable enough to support the weight of heavy specimens and equipment*—If possible, speak with your supervisor about trading your existing furniture for something more suitable. For example, you may find that older furniture, such as oak tables and workbenches from art and industrial arts classrooms, may work better than newer lightweight tables. If ordering new furnishing, opt for standing-height tables with bolted legs reinforced with stretcher bars.

▶ *Hot and cold running water from sinks within the classroom*—If hot water is not available from a central location, get a point-of-use heater under the sink. It's essential for proper sanitation in any science class, but especially where soils are involved.

▶ *Safety eye protection for everyone and a means to disinfect safety eyewear between classes*—Remember that many inquiries on rocks and minerals will require impact-resistant goggles, but the chemical testing will require splash protection, so your eye protection will need to be suitable for both purposes. (See Chapter 10, p. 146, for a detailed discussion on eyewear and eye protection.)

▶ *Secure storage space for chemicals and equipment*—You need a separate chemical storeroom as close as possible to point of use. We recommend that you order prediluted acids in small quantities, so they can be stored in a small, lockable, corrosion-resistant cabinet. You may also need a fire-resistant flammables cabinet for alcohols and lacquers.

▶ *Sufficient space for students to work without bumping one another*—Request that your students leave extraneous supplies in their lockers or provide a storage area away from worktables. Remove chairs and stools from work areas during labs and have students work standing up.

▶ *Ventilation*—Your room should have standard overhead vents to the outside (more than eight exchanges per hour in an occupied lab and four exchanges per hour in an unoccupied lab) plus a fume hood if you use acids or lacquers.

Rock and Roll

Although the National Science Education Standards (NRC 1996) now place more emphasis on cycles and systems, most students will still find their first hands-on experience in Earth science beneath their feet. Rocks and minerals are the most commonly accessible raw materials for inquiry. From them, students learn how to classify and begin to conceptualize the vastness of geologic time.

Because rocks are so familiar, your first challenge is to teach students to respect them as scientific materials. They are heavy and tempting. Give students organizational responsibility such as keeping the heaviest samples on low shelves and making sure boxes and bins are not top-heavy or easily tipped. Although most rock specimens can be stored indefinitely on secure shelving, beware of some specimens that oxidize such as iron ores. The stains can damage nearby surfaces and materials.

Some ores and elements are toxic (e.g., uranium, cobalt), combustible at room temperature (e.g., yellow phosphorus), or unstable (e.g., sodium, potassium) and should not be used or stored in schools. If you still have these items in your school, you might first see if a local museum or university will accept them. Otherwise, you need to request removal by a properly licensed disposal firm. Talc may contain asbestos, so, if you wish to keep a mineral specimen, do not allow it to be scraped or crushed. Do not create, use, or store powdered talc (which may contain asbestos). Talcum powder on the market today is actually starch.

What Part of "No Tasting" Don't You Understand?

Although some geology books or field guides suggest it, rocks should never be tasted for the purpose of identification. Consider the scenario of having students taste a sample of halite to check for a salty taste. Suppose one of the students were an undiagnosed hepatitis carrier, or that the sample was really a heavy metal ore or halite that had been in a box with a chromate. No, don't taste rocks.

Tools of the Trade

Typical Earth science equipment is usually simple, but must be strong and sturdy. As with other science materials, storage must be lockable and secure. But because Earth science equipment tends to be larger and heavier than items for other sciences, storage usually needs to be somewhat roomier and stronger. Because much of the equipment for the Earth sciences is used for cutting or fracturing specimens or obtaining samples under potentially hazardous conditions, you must give students explicit instructions about appropriate as well as safe use. As a general rule, safety eyewear is needed for almost all Earth science activities. Some supplies and equipment suitable for Earth science activities may be available at lower cost from hardware and discount stores. But don't be tempted to cut corners with tools that could break or fracture.

Streak Plates and Other Sharps: Identification of rocks and minerals is an important part of many secondary courses, especially those that use classroom practice to prepare for fieldwork. Because they are made of porcelain, streak plates can break, resulting in extremely sharp shards. Make sure students understand that streak plates must be handled carefully and must be used on a level surface. (See Chapter 10, "Use and Disposal of Sharps," p. 143.)

Rock Hammers: Fracturing rocks is not the same as randomly striking or smashing the specimens. Whether in the field or in the classroom, the process always requires eye protection, direct supervision, and careful selection of the specimen. Choose the rock hammer with care—not just any hammer but one specifically designed for the purpose. This is not a place to save money. Poorly made or improper tools can break during use and cause serious injury. When possible, purchase specimens that show fracture and cleavage rather than fracturing the specimens yourself. Emphasize to students that this is a dangerous, scientifically precise procedure and they should not try it at home or without trained supervision.

Rock Saws: Rock saws are potentially dangerous and not recommended for use in a classroom. They require more attention and preparation than a teacher could give in a whole-class situation. They may be used by a teacher alone or in a small group situation, but students must always be trained and supervised before they use any power tool. You'll need ANSI Z87.1-compliant impact-resistant eye and face protection and gloves, and you will have to make sure your equipment has electric and hand protection.

Rock Tumblers: Rock tumblers may be used in a classroom. They work slowly and use nontoxic grit. The chief problem is that they must be run continuously for extended periods and may be very noisy.

Glues and Lacquers: The standard lacquers used for mineral samples have toxic fumes. You will need a fume hood for drying. Provide students only a very small quantity of the coating material in a well-ventilated area. Eye protection is a must. Make sure you have material safety data sheets (MSDS) on every product you use. (See Chapter 4, p. 52.) Do not use cyanoacrylic glues (e.g., Super Glue) because of their potential for damaging skin and eyes.

Hydrochloric and Other Acids: An acid test is standard for identifying carbonate-containing rocks. A 10% solution of hydrochloric acid (HCl) is sufficient. We strongly recommend that you order prediluted solution in small quantities. The dilution process can be hazardous, and storing concentrated acid represents an unnecessary risk. Store your stock bottle in a locked corrosives cabinet in a secure storeroom. Place small quantities (no more than 10 mL) in labeled dropper bottles before class. Make sure everyone—doers and observers—wears chemical splash safety goggles. Rinse all specimens thoroughly after testing. Remove jet nozzles from faucets to avoid unnecessary splashing.

Heat Sources: Some programs encourage students to dehydrate soil and mineral samples in order to calculate the water content. Microwave ovens work well for these purposes, but do not use the same appliance to heat food for consumption. If you use hot plates, choose those designed for laboratory use, not ones meant for cooking or other household uses. Bunsen burners are seldom needed in Earth and space science. If you do need this level of heat, check Chapter 6, p. 89, for precautions.

Field and Stream Equipment: Packing for field trips is both an art and a science. In the field, you will need all of the safety equipment that you need in the classroom—eye protection, MSDS information, secure storage, and sanitation facilities. Use the smallest possible quantities, pack them securely, and make sure everything is counted before leaving the field site. Choose plastic over glass whenever possible.

For water-related activities, make sure you have water safety equipment, such as life jackets, in the amounts and types required and that everyone is properly instructed on correct use. (See Chapter 9 for additional information.)

Telescopes, Binoculars, and Optical Instruments: These are delicate and expensive instruments and require careful selection and handling. At the high school level, students may be able to handle sensitive equipment, but they will still need complete instructions and safety reminders. The most tempting and dangerous error is observation of the Sun. See p. 102 for special precautions.

Weather Equipment: Today's weather equipment is largely electronic, but you might find older instruments containing mercury (e.g., thermometers, barometers, hygrometers, sling psychrometers). These should be handled as hazardous waste items and should not be used.

The Dirt on Dirt

Although most people associate geology with rocks, the basic scientific material for that course is soil. To study soil appropriately, you need to know the potential hazards in this ubiquitous natural material. Just because it's everywhere doesn't mean it's harmless.

Obtain your soil samples from a source you know, and make sure animal wastes or toxins have not contaminated them. Be sure to research your study site. Industry that existed long ago may be a source of contamination today. Old smelter sites are not uncommon and pose very serious lead contamination risks. Old chemical factories or industrial processes may have impregnated the soil with organics and other chemicals that remain at dangerous levels. One of the most common contaminants of outdoor sites is lead paint dust from nearby buildings, bridges, and other structures that have been scraped and repainted.

Soils are also laced with molds, bacteria, and other potential pathogens. Although the ideal soil for safety is presterilized, it doesn't work for many lessons about naturally occurring communities of organisms. Therefore you must ensure students wash their hands after they have examined the organisms in their samples. If you are testing soils in the classroom, wash the desktops too. But don't expose students to strong disinfectants that can result in irritation and skin breaks. In most cases, soap and water will do, or, in the field, try the newer hand-cleaning gels made of quick-drying

7

alcohol formulations, keeping their flammability in mind. A room used for soil studies should not be used for preparing or consuming food.

Many standard soil laboratories involve the culture of pathogenic bacteria. Winogradsky columns breed both aerobic and anaerobic bacteria. Students should use good hygiene when engaging in such studies, and the contents should be sterilized before disposal.

Other protocols involve isolating certain bacteria from soil cultures. In these situations students may be exposed to pathogens, including *E. coli*, *B. anthracis*, and *C. tetani*. We do not recommend culturing soil bacteria in open culture systems at the high school level. The potential for infection and mold contamination of the classroom is too high. Systems closed with Petrifilm or similar materials may be good substitutes for mature classes. See Chapter 5, p. 70, for more information.

Wet and Wild

Stream tables and ripple tanks provide models of erosion and waves that help students understand what they see in the field. Although they take up a lot of space, they encourage patient observation. Make sure your stream table or ripple tank is securely mounted so it can't tip. You'll need lights for students to see the action, but lights usually mean electricity. Keep your light sources high and secure. Be sure that no one can put one hand in the water and one on the light or splash water onto the hot lights causing them to explode.

Seeing Stars

Astronomy is an ideal science for teaching the skills that established our methods of science—accurate observation, careful record keeping, and proposing new models of the universe. With a few precautions, astronomy can provide a safe and exciting curriculum.

Don't ever let your students observe the Sun directly. Your first lesson might inform students that Galileo lost his eyesight because he didn't understand the danger. The lens of the human eye concentrates solar rays in the same way that a hand lens does. Just as a magnifying lens can focus enough heat energy from the Sun to burn a hole in a piece of paper, so if you look directly at the Sun, the lens of your eye can focus enough of the Sun's rays to burn a hole in your retina and cause permanent eye damage. Sunglasses do not provide protection for looking at the Sun, and using layers of exposed photographic film is a method too unreliable to be trusted. Neither should you use the inexpensive filter glasses (with cardboard earpieces) offered by some vendors. There is simply too much

SCI*LINKS*
THE WORLD'S A CLICK AWAY

Topic: astronomy
Go to: *www.scilinks.org*
Code: SHL102

temptation for students to cheat by looking around these toy goggles. Teach students the pinhole-reflection method of observing solar eclipses.

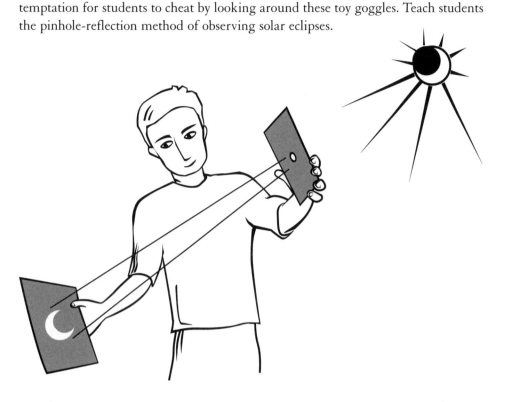

If you are lucky enough to have a telescope or the opportunity to take students to a telescope facility, star-gazing activities will likely require a nighttime or evening field trip. Refer to Chapter 9 for information about field trips. But don't think of astronomy as limited to nighttime activities. Many interesting activities that track the movement of heavenly bodies can be performed during the day. Remember the Sun casts shadows that change size, shape, and placement depending on its position relative to the object casting the shadow. Just make sure you take precautions to prevent overexposure to the Sun if you carry on outdoor astronomy activities in daytime. Under certain conditions, the Moon can be seen in daylight.

Modeling Craters

One often-used lab has students throwing small objects (such as peas) into flour or using plaster of Paris to model craters. As with all projectile activities, these require eye protection. Do not use talc.

7

In the Field

The study of Earth processes can begin in the schoolyard. Observing the playground, the school building, and the sidewalks will reveal examples of erosion and weathering.

A school ground field trip requires the same rules for proper behavior in a field study as a distant one. Before you go, discuss the proper way to travel; prohibitions against running, jumping, and shoving; and the proper way to carry equipment.

Geology and other Earth science fieldwork may require even more planning and advance work than other science field trips, but a well-planned field study can be memorable and inspire students for a lifetime. Protective gear is usually required. Depending on the site, hard leather shoes with toe protection and ankle support may be needed. If you have students who don't own anything but athletic shoes, you may need to make special arrangements to borrow, rent, or otherwise obtain the correct footwear for everyone. You may also need to use protective headgear. Physical conditioning may be necessary. If so, consider working out a training plan with the physical education teachers, and be sure everyone who goes has completed the required training. If you have students with disabilities, you may also need to work with the special education team and school medical staff to ensure they can participate to the fullest extent possible.

If you are conducting activities in or near water, water safety and swimming instruction may be needed. Here, too, the physical education department may be a good partner for your activities.

See Chapter 9, p. 117, "The Great Outdoors," for more information on field trips.

Golden Opportunities

When you teach Earth and space sciences, you help students see the world around them with a more discerning and understanding eye. Your Earth and space science lessons present an authentic way to connect school lessons with out-of-school explorations. After their lessons with you, your students may never whiz past a road cut, mountain, desert, or shoreline, view a quarry or the night sky, or explore a cave in the same way again.

Some travel and vacation adventures may be accompanied by inherent dangers that can be mitigated by lessons learned in your classes and during your fieldwork experiences. When traveling with family and friends, your well-instructed Earth science students will know how to help everyone explore more safely in rugged outdoor environments. Don't teach safety lessons as just a set of rules but rather as a way of doing things in everyday life.

In years to come, your students may be shooting the rapids or flying over irrigated fields applying the knowledge you provided in your classroom and just outside the window. They'll do it safely if you model good habits. So dress yourself in a little common sense and dig in.

THE SAVVY SCIENCE TEACHER

Ms. D's students have rafted white water, climbed mountain peaks, and dived to incredible depths—much of it courtesy of the United States government. They are carried to these virtual adventures on the wings of satellites using the images and data made available to all citizens by agencies such as the National Oceanic and Atmospheric Administration (NOAA), the United States Geological Survey (USGS), and the National Aeronautics and Space Administration (NASA).

Satellite images and other materials also help Ms. D and her classes plan for fieldwork. Before each field experience, her class uses quadrant maps from the U.S. Geological Survey, satellite images from NASA, and other data to identify physical features, potential hazards, and challenges of the proposed field site, and to plan "what if" scenarios to mitigate problems well before the actual trip.

Other data and maps reveal overhead and buried power lines, water courses, and navigation electronics. Some satellite images can even show the moisture content of forest and grassland sites to assist in determining the fire hazard level of prospective field sites.

All this vicarious adventuring helps Ms. D's students get more out of their actual field studies, because once they arrive at a real field site, they know what to expect and waste little time getting to the task of making observations and recording data.

When the field trip is over, Ms. D's students hit the satellite again. They upload their data to the Internet, to share with fellow student researchers around the world.

7

Connections

▶ The Microbial World. See *helios.bto.ed.ac.uk/ bto/microbes/ winograd.htm.*
▶ National Aeronautics and Space Administration. See *www.nasa.gov.*

▶ National Oceanic and Atmospheric Administration. See *www.nooa.gov.*
▶ U.S. Geological Survey. See *www.usgs.gov.*

Falling for Science

Physics Phenoms

Somewhere in your school community, there's a tinkerer who dreams of launching a rocket, a mechanic designing a racer in a page margin, a stagehand mixing lights for a play, a sound technician with music reverberating from ear to ear. Each is a scientist at heart. It's our job to show them how the laws of physics play a role in some of their favorite phenomena.

Not Elitist Anymore

There was once a time when physics students were the elite of the elite—mostly the top college-bound seniors with a driving interest in science and simultaneously enrolled in advanced placement mathematics. Today, we believe that all students deserve to stand, as Newton said he did, "on the shoulders of giants." Many schools offer excellent grade 9 and 10 conceptual physics classes with minimal mathematics requirements; others provide interdisciplinary physics programs with lessons on the history and methods of science along with investigative physics. Sometimes vocational education teachers teach applied physics. These efforts are aimed at providing a broad range of students with a solid understanding of the basic laws of nature. They also mean that physics teachers must adjust curricula to meet the needs of these students. Teaching methods and safety instruction must also be adjusted to ensure full and safe participation by all.

8

Perpetual Motion

The bell rings. Students crowd in. Amid the specialized tools of physical scientists, force and motion are hard to avoid. Everything about the subject promises action. Sitting on shelves or counters, the gauges and machines capture the imagination of students. You know that part of your job is to see to it that your students learn how to use these instruments properly. Air tracks and dynamics carts look a lot like toys. Geiger counters and oscilloscopes might be mistaken for video games. Improper use can be both dangerous and expensive.

Cars and driving are major goals of high school students. Unfortunately, the auto crash rates are higher for teens than any other age group. Lecturing about auto safety seems to have a very limited effect. However, physics classes and real data collection may offer another means of communicating with young drivers. Can your lessons on force and motion, momentum, and inertia make a difference?

Pay attention to the real-world applications that students may want to explore when they learn the laws of motion. Take special care when you plan activities with materials that swing, rotate, speed, or drop from the sky. Just because physics students can calculate how long it will take for a ball to fall from the roof of the gymnasium doesn't mean that they should be climbing up there. There's a big difference between understanding the forces acting on a car and appropriately directing the forces to keep the car in control. Not every amusement park ride is safe and educational. But with careful planning, each of these experiences can provide great application exercises in physics.

Never overestimate your students' understanding of the dangers of real-world physics. They are at an age when caution rises and falls like a roller coaster. Remember that you may be liable for accidents and errors in judgment that result from your classroom stories. So if you describe a dangerous stunt that might illustrate some physics principle in class, it won't be enough to simply say, "Don't try this." If you can't engage students in sufficient discussion to ensure that they won't try the stunt, ditch the story.

Sights and Sounds

To many high school students, *sound* is what's blasted through headsets, *light* is the flashes of a concert strobe, and "*the wave*" is a group activity. As you expand your students' view, take the opportunity to instill a little healthy caution.

Many teachers encourage students to make their own sound generators or musical instruments. If you do so, make sure that percussion instruments can't shatter, string instruments can't break and send parts flying, and wind instruments don't spread germs.

Once high schoolers discover that sound is science, take the opportunity to consider a lesson on noise. Hearing damage caused by sound that is loud or constant, or both, is a growing problem among young people. They use headsets, boom boxes, and other sources of loud music and sound without realizing the extent of permanent damage that can be done to their hearing. Learning to use decibel meters and other measurement devices can not only ensure safety in your classroom but help students build better listening habits for life. The "high speed siren" apparatus often used to demonstrate sound must be firmly installed (check the safety nut) and used only at moderate speed in class. You should not be generating sound loud enough to require hearing protection for yourself or your students.

If you have your students measure and calculate the speed of sound on campus, some students may be placed at some distances across campus with noisemakers and timing devices. The experience may be good but the temptations are also great. Spend time planning a way to monitor all the students and making sure they understand their responsibility when working in the field.

It's not just a movie trick. Tuning forks and other sound-generating devices can shatter glass. Provide clear directions and cautions when using these seemingly simple devices. When studying resonance, a little tape on the top of a glass tube reduces the risk of shattering. Impact-resistant safety eyewear is a must. Ripple tanks should be set up in a secure place and away from electrical outlets. Lights should be positioned so they can't be splashed with water.

Lasers and laser pointers, black lights, and strobes should be used only with great caution. Provide structured laboratory investigations with specific directions for data collection and appropriate eye protection throughout. Make sure the target for your laser is set up well in advance, is nonreflective and secure. In high school classes, do not exceed 0.5 milliwatts in a helium-neon laser.

If you work with lenses, consider discussions related to the lens of the eye and proper eye protection. Help students understand the dangers of staring directly at any bright light, particularly the Sun. (For additional explanation, see Chapter 7, p. 102, "Seeing Stars.")

Charge Ahead

Electricity is both a tool and an important content area in physics, but the cytosol of the human cell is a great electrolyte, and electric shock is a constant danger in the home or in the classroom. The severity of a shock doesn't depend just upon the voltage, but also upon the current, the body's resistance, and the path the current takes through the body. The median threshold for the smallest current that can be felt is about 5 milliampers (mA) direct current or 1 mA at 60 Hz alternating current (Sarquis 2000). At about 16 mA or more, the muscles of the body freeze, so the victim has no way to pull away or let go. At 23 mA the shock can be fatal. Do not depend on insulating gloves and shoes, or putting one hand in your pocket. The way to resist shock is to avoid it from the outset.

SCI
LINKS.
THE WORLD'S A CLICK AWAY
Topic: electricity
Go to: www.scilinks.org
Code: SHL109

Classrooms in older schools are notoriously short of electrical receptacles, and the ones there tend to be located in all the wrong places. Don't try to solve the problem by using socket multipliers or extension cords. More wire produces more resistance, less usable power, and a greater fire hazard. If you trip a circuit breaker, you don't have enough capacity. Don't try it again—call maintenance.

Outdated Rule

Many older manuals suggest keeping one hand in a pocket to prevent electric current from flowing from one hand, across the chest, and out the other hand when working with appliances. Do not rely on this old trick for protection. Unplug electrical devices before handling them. Stop shocks before they happen.

All outlets should be properly grounded, and outlets near water should be protected with a ground-fault interrupter (GFI). If your room does not have adequate electric service, or if the outlets do not have the proper grounding and safety features, make a request for upgrade or repairs in writing and be sure to include both the educational and safety reasons for your request. Do not perform unsafe activities or use unsafe equipment until the deficiencies have been corrected. Be sure all electrical equipment you use is properly grounded and do not circumvent the ground plug with an adapter "cheater" wire.

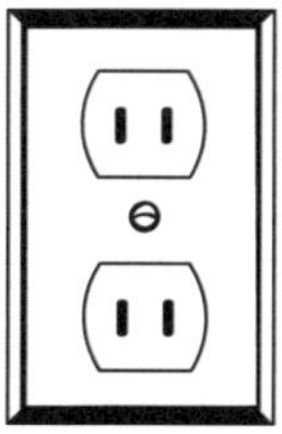

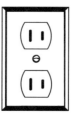

Figure 1

In the United States, typical household receptacles provide 110–120 volts, and come in three types. The oldest type has two equal openings, and plugs can be inserted in any direction (Figure 1). Schools should not still have these in the walls. Newer receptacles have one slot larger than the other (Figure 2). Televisions and some other electrical devices must be plugged in in one direction, not another. The third and preferred form of receptacle has two slots of different sizes and a third opening for a ground pin (Figure 3). The third type is the only form of receptacle that should be in a classroom.

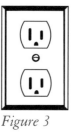

Figure 2

Some devices—such as kilns, stoves, shop equipment, and theater lighting equipment—may require 210–220 volts. The receptacles for these lines are generally round, with large openings arranged radially. The arrangement of the prongs in these plugs correlates to the amperage the tool or appliance will draw. Never try to rewire an appliance with a different type of plug than the one that came with it. The amperage to be carried determines the configuration of the socket, so the appliance must be exactly matched to the receptacle intended for it.

Figure 3

8

Even if you have plenty of the right kinds of electrical receptacles, you may still be challenged to get the power to the right place. (Refer to Chapter 3, p. 36, "Power Up," for information on getting power to the middle of the room.) When you plan the routes for your power cords pay special attention to sinks and water. Never string a cord across a sink or near a water tap. Loosely wrap power cords and place the coil on the equipment. When they are tightly wrapped around the equipment, the cord frays at the point of entry and in time will expose bare wires, then break.

Many people consider batteries and direct current a safer alternative to wall current—and they usually are correct. But be cautious here, too. Don't use rechargeable batteries in series; their voltage can be unpredictable. Do not use automobile or industrial batteries. They may leak acid or explode if shorted. These batteries are not appropriate for student or classroom use.

If you use a voltage transformer/generator for experiments, make sure it cannot generate current that is dangerously high. Also provide clear safety directions to the students. Although the Van de Graaff generator is a time-honored and exciting demonstration, it is also a potential hazard. Treat this voltage generator with respect, and make sure that no student in the demonstration area has a pacemaker or other medical condition that would make the Van de Graaff output potentially dangerous. Never open a television or computer monitor. They have capacitors that may store large charges even when unplugged. Picture tubes and other CRTs (cathode-ray tubes) may implode. Leyden jars and large capacitors can pose serious shock hazards.

APPLYING SAFE ELECTRIC PRACTICE

Encourage your students to become electrical safety experts at home and work as well as in school.

▶ Make sure electrical outlets are not broken and that plugs fit well in them.

▶ Never stick anything into an electrical receptacle or an appliance that is still plugged in—use safety covers on unused receptacles where young children might be present.

▶ Check lightbulbs to make sure the wattage does not exceed the rating of the appliance or wall socket.

▶ Never use multiple extension cords on the same circuit or cover extension cords with floor covering.

▶ If an appliance trips a breaker, turn it off until the appliance is checked.

▶ Keep space heaters at least one meter away from walls and combustible materials.

▶ Keep combustible materials away from halogen lamps.

▶ Never use an electrical appliance near water or electrical tools in the rain.

▶ Do not use adapters that bypass the ground or use plugs that have had the ground pin removed.

For more tips: See the National Electrical Safety Foundation website at *www.esfi.org/index.php.*

8

Tools of the Trade

Physical science equipment ranges from simple tools to sophisticated electrical meters. You need clear, flat surfaces on sturdy tables and counters—longer and wider than the standard types for biology or chemistry. Make sure that legs are fastened to the tabletop with strong bolts and not just glued on. Choose standing-height tables with stretcher reinforcements on the legs. You'll need every bit of 60 ft^2 of working space per student in the physics room. As with all science rooms, the physics location needs eye protection and sterilizing facilities (Chapter 10, p. 146), fire protection (Chapter 3, p. 39), and proper storage and disposal areas (Chapter 4). In older facilities, storage will take creativity, since cabinets and shelves may not be designed for the larger pieces of physics equipment.

Here are some other common items:

▸ **Carpentry Tools:** Hammers, saws, and other carpentry tools can be useful for constructing a variety projects. Make sure everyone is properly instructed in the use of the tools and that everyone, including bystanders, is wearing appropriate eye protection. Choose cutting tools with safety shields and keep them secure when not in use. High school students should use power tools only in the proper setting and after strict safety training. Physics classrooms may lack the space or outlets for power tools. Consider partnering with vocational education instructors when you engage in projects that require the use of power tools.

▸ **Pendulums:** Safely conducting these activities depends on class discipline. Begin with short strings and rounded bobs. Before each use, check, and have your students check, that the bobs are securely fastened to their strings. Encourage careful observation and good record keeping. Teach students to begin the swing by letting go of the pendulum bob rather than pushing or throwing the bob. Impact-resistant eye protection may be needed with pendulums and whirling objects such as used in centripetal acceleration experiments.

▸ **Momentum Carts (cars):** Be aware of the placement of ramps. Make sure they do not block walking paths or send cars zooming into the hall. Be sure cars aren't left out on the floor or any other walking area, and put them away when class changes.

▸ **Carbon Dioxide Pellets:** These can produce significant momentum. Cars using them should be on tracks and not running freely. Use eye protection.

▸ **Model Rockets:** Check the legality of these devices in your district. Use only approved engines and electric igniters. During construction, make sure the cardboard ring that holds the rocket engine during launch is glued in straight. Erratic, dangerous flights can ensue otherwise. Students launching rockets must be supervised and must wear eye protection.

▸ **Balances:** Keep them secure. They are highly valued for illicit drug activity.

- **Manometers:** Any equipment that contains elemental mercury should be retired. The mercury they contain must be treated as hazardous waste. (Refer to Chapter 6, p. 87.)

- **Siren Disks:** Make sure the safety nut is securely fastened and use only at moderate speed.

- **Van de Graaff Generators, Leyden Jars, Large Capacitors:** Consider eliminating these items. (See this chapter, p. 109, "Charge Ahead.")

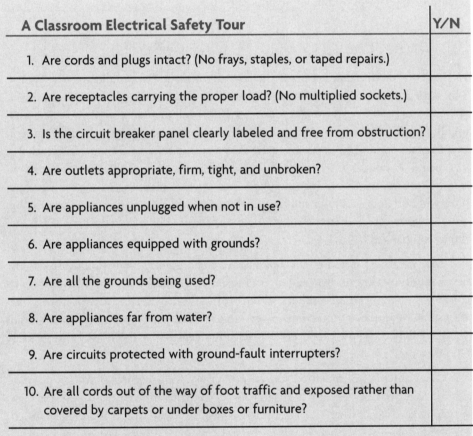

A Classroom Electrical Safety Tour	Y/N
1. Are cords and plugs intact? (No frays, staples, or taped repairs.)	
2. Are receptacles carrying the proper load? (No multiplied sockets.)	
3. Is the circuit breaker panel clearly labeled and free from obstruction?	
4. Are outlets appropriate, firm, tight, and unbroken?	
5. Are appliances unplugged when not in use?	
6. Are appliances equipped with grounds?	
7. Are all the grounds being used?	
8. Are appliances far from water?	
9. Are circuits protected with ground-fault interrupters?	
10. Are all cords out of the way of foot traffic and exposed rather than covered by carpets or under boxes or furniture?	

Source: Sarquis (2000).

The Computer Age

Computers have added a new level of challenge to classroom design. Classrooms designed and built prior to the use of computers almost never have sufficient electrical service in needed locations. Surge protectors and universal power sources (UPS) are needed to protect valuable and sensitive computer equipment from power surges and outages.

Computers and related equipment also require additional space. They should not be placed near sinks and should be spaced far enough apart so students can use them without interfering with other equipment and each other. If your room isn't equipped with sufficient power in the appropriate locations for full desktop computers, consider laptops. The batteries that are used for computers and calculators are usually specialized for the use and the device. If they can be recharged, follow the instructions exactly and use the supplied recharger. Do not mix these batteries with those used for science investigations and other activities.

Radiating Energy

High school physics courses often include a unit on radiation and nuclear energy. This is an important component of a twenty-first century course. Teachers are justifiably eager to provide hands-on experiences with radiation to help student understanding. But laboratory activities using radioactive materials may pose hazards to students as well as the community at large. Some students may have read about the creation of so-called dirty bombs and become inappropriately fascinated with material you consider to be a routine laboratory supply. When you are planning hands-on investigations with radiation, it's important to consider not only what you want to happen, but also the worst-case scenario of what might happen if your materials were to fall into the wrong hands.

Many teachers store low-level alpha, beta, and gamma radiation sources to use in laboratory studies on penetration and distance. If you do so, you will have to be concerned not only about student use, but also about disposal and security. Store only very small quantities of materials in very secure facilities, even though the materials you have may be below the levels that require licensure by the Nuclear Regulatory Commission (NRC).

Using any level of radiation source in the classroom requires thorough preparation. It may well be potentially dangerous to students and may also pose the most serious hazards to staff who have repeated exposure. Great care and caution should be followed if older sources are found in the stock room or other places. They may well be left over from earlier times when nuclear material was easily available. Don't assume. Unless you know for certain what the source is and its qualities, treat it as dangerous. As general rule, any source that is unknown, inadequately labeled, or obviously a leftover from earlier times should not be used. Isolate and secure it until appropriate assistance can be found to properly remove it.

No unprepared visitor or student can be near the classroom during the laboratory. Students must be thoroughly prepared in advance. You'll have to be specific about what they wear, what they bring to class, and what they do when they are there. Designated gloves and tongs (reserved only for that purpose) should be used and stored separately. You must make specific arrangements for disposal and cleanup and have secure storage that *no one else* in the school community can access.

It is rare that a high school physics teacher can mitigate the radiation safety concerns, making it doubtful that radioactive materials can be used safely in a high school classroom today.

There are many significant activities that students do to investigate radiation. Cosmic background radiation is measurable with most classroom Geiger counters. Students may be surprised to discover radiation sources in smoke detectors (americium) and in the basements and well water of homes (radon). Commonly found items may also be low-level sources of radiation suitable for high school laboratory demonstrations. Different found rocks and granite used to make countertops may be usable low-level radiation sources. Students may be fascinated by the true story of glow-in-the-dark watch-dial painters exposed to lethal radiation from licking their brushes (radium). They can learn from examining X-rays, crystallography, and other products of nuclear science. Many medical and industrial professionals are glad to share what they do with your students and even to guide field trips.

THE SAVVY SCIENCE TEACHER

Ms. T's physics students are also performers. The highlight of their work each year is a "Physics Extravaganza" that becomes a traveling show for their neighboring elementary schools.

Each extravaganza begins with a light show. But this one involves student participation. As each stage strobe is added to the display, children predict the results and learn about light mixing.

The heart of the show involves magic tricks. Students pull tablecloths out from under fine china, turn virtual objects upside down with lenses and mirrors, and change sounds by waving their hands. For each trick they perform on stage, they provide the host teacher with their own explanation of the physics behind the fun.

Proud inventors display their self-built musical instruments and accompany the show with familiar songs on very unfamiliar devices.

After each show, Ms. T's students join the elementary kids on the playground and share physics secrets there, too.

8

Connections

▶ American Association of Physics Teachers. *Safety in physics education.* 2002. College Park, MD: AAPT. See Products Catalog at *www.aapt. org/store/products. cfm?ShowAll=1.*

▶ The International Electrical Safety Foundation. See *www.esfi.org/index.php.*

▶ McCullough, J., and R. McCullough. 2000. *The role of toys in teaching physics.* College Park, MD: American Association of Physics Teachers.

▶ Physics Safety Issues. The Catalyst. See *www.the catalyst.org/hwrp/ safetymanual/ physics.html.*

▶ Sarquis, M. 2000. *Building student safety habits for the workplace.* Middletown, OH: Terrific Science Press.

8

The Great Outdoors

Field Studies Near and Far

The decision to schedule field trips and field studies at the high school level is often a struggle between competing interests. You must weigh the value of gathering data and experiences that cannot be acquired in the classroom against the disruption of your colleagues' curricula by removing substantial numbers of their students. You should also think about the possible scenarios that can result from taking dozens of emerging adolescents into an informal setting. Will your students appear as eager learners or bored know-it-alls, avid budding scientists or smart alecks looking to stump the docent, model citizens or escaped prisoners eager for a surreptitious smoke? Most teachers who include fieldwork as an integral part of their program can easily explain why they are willing to put in the hours of extra planning to make these field experiences work well for their students. And there are hundreds of stories of students inspired by a field experience that has marked the beginning of a lifelong interest and career in science. As with every other type of science lesson, the difference between success and failure and between a safe, memorable learning experience and disaster is a matter of careful planning and preparation.

Classroom Limits

Most twenty-first century high school students move and think way beyond the limits of their classrooms and schools. They drive, or ride with friends, and explore beyond the limits of their communities long after their teachers are fast asleep. Mentally, they move between the concrete and the abstract with sometimes bewildering swiftness. They should also have acquired a lot of basic science skills and concepts that allow them to observe, measure, and relate with some degree of reliability. It is time to move them beyond the school and into other settings where science principles can be applied and expanded.

But high school students also lack caution and believe in their own immortality. They often find field trip rules stifling—especially when they are visiting places they may have seen independently. It may be a challenge to set and enforce rules on high school field trips. But for the sake of safety and continuity, you must.

9

A Journey of a Thousand Miles ...

Despite the fact that your high school students seem like savvy travelers, it's still a good idea to choose venues close to the school for your first fieldwork. If you are going to engage in direct data collection in the field, begin with field collection close to the school and choose activities that can be completed within a single lab period.

Practice structured fieldwork with progressively longer and more complex tasks. Practice field skills in local settings such as the schoolyard or local playing field before setting out to a more distant location. Start with a simulation. Many websites offer great practice. Then hone your students' skills, so that your major fieldwork trip(s) garner reliable data. Here are some local field studies you might assign:

▶ Survey biota in microenvironments around the high school using quadrat analysis.

▶ Gather materials for soil analysis from the lawns and plant beds around the school or the high school field.

▶ Use school records and photographs such as yearbook archives to compare the relative effects of weather on metal bleacher components, bicycle stands, and building joists.

▶ Find the number of moles of sidewalk chalk required to write your name in 10-cm high letters.

▶ Observe the momentum and inertia of children on the neighboring elementary playground equipment before the field trip to the amusement park.

Even if your trip is just to the football field, remember that all students must be under your direct supervision. If a tardy student appears after safety instructions, make sure he or she gets those instructions or makes up the fieldwork at a later time. Arrange a stop-work, cleanup signal that accounts for properly gathering all equipment and returning to the building on time. Let students know they are responsible for being at their next classes on time. Warn them you are not going to issue late passes for the next class.

Before engaging in long-distance or overnight travel, try a trip to a local informal science center (such as a museum or nature center) to introduce students to focused exhibit viewing and the expectations and etiquette of visiting out. Most museums and centers have webpages, so you can involve your students in pretrip planning activities. Instill in students the sense that further fieldwork depends on their seriousness of purpose and conduct. Focus on group integrity and personal responsibility and that each person has a commitment to the group and a responsibility to self. The students should protect the field activity not only as something they would want to do again but also for others in succeeding classes.

9

Preview and Prepare

It is imperative that you preview and thoroughly examine any field site you are considering. You need to take the trip ahead of time with tentative plans and a thorough checklist to find the potential hazards you never would have thought of while looking at the site's website or reading program literature. Then write your final plans, including safety preparations, chaperone training, permission slip modifications specific to your trip, clothing and gear requirements, and schedules for travel, work, and site cleanup.

Depending on the topography of the site, you must also plan a method for monitoring where each student is, what students are doing, and calling all students together at designated times and in emergencies. A teacher frantically blowing a whistle, yelling, or giving last-minute behavior instructions in the field, while students scatter like first-year calves through a hole in the fence, is not indicative of a prepared field trip. The class is not ready for a trip until everyone knows what behavior is expected even when the unexpected occurs. Put particular emphasis on the rule that no one may leave the site and his or her assigned location without your explicit permission. Anyone missing must be reported immediately, and all other work must stop until the missing person is located.

If you expect to use staff or consultants from the field site, then a full and detailed planning session should include a discussion of exactly how you will prepare your students, what you expect your partner and consultants to do with your students, and enough information about your group and individual students for the outsider to know what to expect and how to work safely and effectively with your class. Don't assume that, just because your guides are experts in technology, wild plants, or rock outcrops, they understand adolescents. A good planning conference is worth its time in gold.

Make sure you have written permission to be at your site and to do what you plan to do. If you are visiting public lands and working with plants or animals, be sure you have all the permission and permits necessary. Some plants and animals are listed as endangered and may not be disturbed.

Stakeholders

Before embarking on any trip, every student (and every student's parents) must be thoroughly informed of expectations and agree to abide by rules of behavior for the trip. Consequences for infractions must also be agreed upon ahead of time.

Make students and their parents stakeholders in the trip so they will work to protect both the trip and the site. If permission must be obtained from local authorities such as the school board, have students assist with the presentation. If the success and continuation of the field experience depends upon commitments students have made publicly, so much the better.

9

Despite their apparent sophistication, high school students need structure on a field trip. Establish groups, with specific group responsibilities, in advance. Whether you need an adult with each group will depend upon the site. With a class of responsible students at an indoor environment such as an aquarium, you might assign groups to work at assignments independently if you have specific, prearranged check-ins and rendezvous. But a trip to a geologic site is likely to be too tempting for daredevils to have anything but direct adult supervision for all groups at all times. If you have students who may present a danger to themselves or others, then consideration must be given to whether the proposed field trip should take place or wait for another year.

Though students may be assigned to work in small groups, for added safety, you should pair students and ask that each member of the pair be responsible for keeping his or her "buddy" in sight at all times. In the excitement of activities, an individual student might not be missed even in a small group. This buddy system is especially important for any field studies at or near bodies of water.

Who's in Charge?

In the same way that you structure a class period, structure your field experiences. Give points or specific consequences for reporting at prearranged points and times. Set up your group procedures so mutual responsibility among group members is built in. In planning activities, embed self-monitoring activities that require students to come together at frequent intervals to share and record data and make a contribution to the group before proceeding further. For example, on a paper worksheet or electronic database, require reports from every member of the group before going on to the next data collection task.

As discussed in Chapter 1, keep in mind that you are responsible for everything that is done with your class at all times. That is key to recognizing the steps you need to take in preparing for a field trip. Even though there are extra adults, remember it is your responsibility to thoroughly prepare your assistants for their duties. Do not invite or accept any other person's assistance in your class and with your students unless you have reviewed the entire plan, purpose, and procedure for the activity and assured yourself that your helper is fully qualified to provide responsible assistance. An extra adult who is "not with the program" becomes another major responsibility—select your helpers carefully.

Students may be carrying cell phones, but, during the trip, they should be used for emergencies only. In no case should students be using them for chatting during the trip or using them to arrange to meet with others not involved with your trip. Your field trip should be reserved for your students only—no guests.

9

HOW MANY IS ENOUGH?

There is no clear ratio of adults to students that can be applied to fieldwork. The right number depends on such disparate factors as the distance and location of the site, the hazards at the site, the nature of the activities you have planned, the skill and experience of the chaperones, and the behavior of the students in your class. However, here are some guidelines to help:

▶ Do not count yourself in the adult-student ratio or assign yourself to a specific group. You need to be available to monitor the overall activity and support your helpers.

▶ Do not count special education aides in the adult-student ratio. In groups with special education students, the aide(s) or coteacher should be an addition to the subgroup chaperone.

▶ If a student has a record of being disruptive, you must make arrangements for appropriate monitoring such as described in an individual education plan (IEP). In some cases you might need to exclude a student from the trip. But progressive discipline consistent with district policy and any relevant IEP provisions must be clearly documented. Work closely with your administration and special education staff before the event.

▶ Never take a trip without at least one other chaperone, no matter how well supervised the site is. If there were an accident or a student got lost, you would need someone for the large group and someone to handle the emergency.

▶ Make sure you conform to any adult or student policies required by school authorities.

Whatever the number of adult chaperones, students should understand they are responsible for monitoring their own behavior and each other's.

How Are You Going to Get There?

Students should never be allowed to drive to field trip sites themselves. If you were to allow such a trip, you would become responsible for the students' driving and your insurance could become primary in case of accident. Parents may find their insurance would not cover driving for a school field trip, either. Use chartered or school buses or prearranged public transportation.

To Go or Not to Go

What to do with the disruptive student whose behavior you do not trust in an out-of-classroom environment? There is no simple answer for this. The factors are many:

▶ What is the history of the behavior problems? Is it better or worse under certain conditions, and how do the conditions compare with the conditions you expect in your fieldwork?

▶ What is your school/ district policy? Are administrators willing to provide additional personnel—perhaps themselves—to accompany this student?

▶ Is this a problem documented in an individual education plan (IEP) for the student? If so, what are the recommendations and special provisions?

▶ Have you discussed the student's behavior with the parents or guardians? Are they willing to cooperate and support your recommendations? Are the parents willing to give you the authority and resources to send

(cont. next page)

Public transportation—buses, trains, trams, trolleys, subways, ferries—may be an economical option. But don't assume your students know how to navigate through a public transportation system. And remember that keeping a large group together for boarding and disembarking is significantly more complex than with individuals or small groups. Check explicitly to make sure the transportation system is prepared to accommodate your group—the regularly scheduled run may not have enough room for more than a few extra passengers. Make sure you review embarking and disembarking instructions with students and chaperones. Provide explicit instructions for what to do if someone is left on the platform or in the vehicle.

If you use buses, be sure you provide each bus driver and the transportation supervisor with written plans that include:

▶ names and number of passengers (adults and students)

▶ destination and drop-off location at the trip site

▶ field site departure time

Each vehicle should have aboard an adult chaperone or student in charge who is responsible for taking attendance on that vehicle before each departure. Do not permit students to change vehicles during the trip. The vehicle you are on should be the last to depart from any site.

If you are planning walking or hiking, make sure all participants are appropriately conditioned and that their footwear is appropriate. Whether traveling in small or large groups, the slowest walker or hiker should be at the lead and a designated person at the rear should check in regularly to ensure the group stays together.

Expected time of return should be clearly stated on the trip permission slip, and parents and guardians should be asked to indicate what arrangement has been made for the student upon return. When you return, make sure all students are picked up or sent home according to the arrangement specified on the permission slip before you leave the school. Prior to departure, establish a telephone chain for informing the school and all parents/guardians in the event of changes in plans or a delay in the return to school.

Museums, Zoos, and More

A visit to an informal science center is most effective when advance preparation is thorough. The most productive and the safest of such visits have a narrowly focused purpose that has been carefully discussed in advance with the educational staff of the institution to be visited. The facility may have worksheets or preplanned exercises you can modify. If not, visit first and develop your own.

Preparatory classroom work before the visit is important. The greatest potential for disappointment and trouble arises when the visits are general tours, or when the teacher simply turns students over to the institution staff. You cannot turn over your responsibility for the behavior and well being of your students to some other person. If students do not have a specific series of tasks to complete and objectives that are an integral part of your school program, they can be easily tempted to race through the site, cause disturbances, harm exhibits, or leave without permission.

To Go (cont.)

the student home midtrip if the behavior is unacceptable?
▶ What provisions can be in place for immediate intervention and sending the student home if things do not work out?
▶ What is the potential effect of this student's behavior on the rest of the students? Can you guarantee protecting everyone else if this student becomes disruptive?
It may be legal to exclude a behaviorally challenged student from a field trip, but it is always necessary to lay out the rules, the consequences, and the potential appeal processes in advance.

With a clear focus, students are much less likely to amuse themselves in unproductive or dangerous ways. Your presence and participation with the institution's instructors are also imperative to connect the field site experience with classroom work. You are the one who knows your students best, and you are responsible for knowing exactly what they have been taught and what they have experienced, even if you are not the lead instructor.

9

Outdoor Sites

Whether the site is as near as just outside the school doors or far enough away to require a bus or an overnight stay, you need to check out the possible hidden hazards, especially if you are using an unfamiliar location. You should also make sure the site does not carry restrictions for use and access. Ask for written permission to do your studies on the site. Check this particularly with conservation land, wildlife preserves, and private property, and make sure there is no hazardous materials contamination.

We Have Met the Enemy and They Are Us

If there is a structure such as a bridge or tower near your chosen site, expect temptation. Do not count on students to read and obey "Danger, Keep Out" signs. Be clear and specific. You should also find out if there have been refurbishing projects that could have taken lead paint off the structure and allowed lead dust to contaminate the area. If utilities have right-of-ways in or near a site, identify any high voltage hazards. Sites near utilities and manufacturing and research facilities should be checked for the possibility of toxic wastes. Areas formerly used for military training may contain unspent munitions. Turn these possible hazards into a safety learning experience, and do not use any site unless you can be certain that you can keep students a safe distance from hazards.

Water, Water, Everywhere

Some of the most common extended field trips in high schools involve water sampling. Check your site in advance. What is the footing like near the water's edge? Is the water biologically or chemically contaminated? Will there be mosquitoes? Are there snakes, alligators, snapping turtles, or other potentially harmful organisms? Is the water deep enough that you'll need water safety equipment and clothing such as waders and gloves? Remember, students can drown in very shallow water if they are careless or unsupervised. Regulation life preservers should be on and not just available. In the worst case, who would be responsible for water rescue or CPR (cardiopulmonary resuscitation)? For trips that require using a boat, make sure the operators of each vessel meet all licensing, safety, and insurance standards and requirements. Students should not be permitted to operate boats.

9

Water studies may use chemicals or probes. All equipment used on a field trip should be tested in the classroom first. Practice the procedures in advance. Incorporate responsibility for maintaining and operating the equipment in group tasks and procedures. If you use chemicals, you will need to bring material safety data sheets (MSDS) along with the kits.

Establish rules for where samples may be collected and the depth of the water in which students can explore for them. For any work in tidal zones, students must wear proper life jackets and be tied to an anchored point on shore if possible. Do not tolerate any infractions.

An Animal's Home Is Its Castle

In the field, your students will trespass into the habitats of animals. Teach them to respect these homes and the ecosystems they visit. Prepare by asking questions and perhaps assigning reading and research in ethology: What animals are likely to be found at or near your site? What is the normal behavior of these animals? What are signs that the animal may be sick or injured? You do not have to be the expert, but you do need to check with a naturalist or guide who is familiar with the location and can advise you thoroughly and accurately.

As a rule, students should not approach any animal—living or dead. The normal behavior of animals is to hide or run from humans. One that approaches your group or does not scurry away is more likely to be sick or injured and should be left alone. Teach students to avoid nests or dens: They are likely to be the home of fleas or other populations best left where they are. An animal protecting its young is likely to be very aggressive. Above all, do not touch or approach a sick or injured animal—do not attempt a rescue or try to bring it back to your classroom. This is usually illegal. (See Chapter 5, p. 74.)

Rocks and logs provide shelter for many organisms. A single rock or log may be home to dozens of plant and animal species that may live in, on, or under the object. Students should be instructed not to disturb these habitats or, if examining them, to exercise care to limit movement and exposure and to be certain to return the object exactly to its original position. A class traversing a beach or forest carelessly kicking, rolling, and lifting rocks or logs can be devastating to the inhabitants.

You need to be aware of insects that are indigenous to the area and whether they could carry infectious human disease (e.g., Lyme disease, Rocky Mountain spotted fever, West Nile virus, Eastern equine encephalitis, hantavirus, dengue fever, or malaria). Check

> ## Marine Microcosms
> The surfaces of rocks on marine beaches provide many habitats. Organisms making their homes on the top are different from those found on the sides or bottom. After lifting a rock to inspect its population, return it in exactly the same way it was found—top up and bottom down. A class carelessly lifting and dropping rocks can destroy a beach's living systems.

9

with your district medical services if you have any questions or doubts. To ensure that allergies and personal preferences are treated appropriately, ask parents and guardians to supply insect repellents for students where needed. Students need to understand the repellents they use may affect others, and so they must apply them sparingly and away from others. Check with the district medical authority as to the potential toxicity of repellents that contain DEET. Determine whether anyone on the trip has allergies to bee stings or other insect bites and what you are required to do about it. See Chapter 10, "First Aid," p. 142, for information about using EpiPens to forestall an anaphylactic reaction.

Parsley, Sage, Rosemary, and Thyme

Vegetation in an outdoor area can also pose hazards. Remind students in writing that nothing should be tasted or eaten.

Pollen and spores may cause allergic responses. Be sure to check for allergic sensitivities among your students and assistants. If you have sensitized students, you may want to avoid outdoor activities altogether when pollen and mold counts are high.

Plants can cause serious irritation on contact. The best known are members of the *Rhus* family, commonly called poison ivy, poison oak, poison sumac, and poison elder. These plants are widespread in outdoor areas and may have different appearances in different habitats and seasons. Learn how to identify them and teach your chaperones and students to do the same. If you expect to encounter *Rhus* species on your trip, carry products that can be applied immediately if skin contact is made with the plants.

Some people mistakenly believe they are immune to the irritants in these plants because they have come into contact with poison ivy or its relatives without developing the classic itching and blistering response. In fact, sensitivity to the antigens can develop as a result of a series of exposures, with each subsequent contact resulting in a stronger response.

9

Some Common Toxic Plants

poison ivy

poison oak

oleander

hemlock

poison sumac

9

The saps of many plants are serious irritants, particularly milky-looking saps. Students should be taught to avoid touching plants they are unfamiliar with and to wash off thoroughly following accidental contact. Be sure to warn against rubbing of eyes that may transfer substances from the hands to the eyes.

Campfires have sometimes been included in overnight trips. However, current practice is to avoid such an activity. The safety issues include the potential of accidentally starting an uncontrolled fire and the production of highly toxic fumes if the wrong wood or twigs, such as oleander or *Rhus*, are included.

The Sun Also Rises

Bronzy tanned skin has traditionally been associated with health, vigor, and glamour. Teens are no exception to those who seek natural and salon exposure to cultivate deep tans. But we now know there is reason for serious concern about skin damage caused by ultraviolet (UV) radiation during sun exposure. Excessive UV exposure when young can greatly increase the risk of skin cancers years later, and recent data show an alarming emergence of melanoma in teenagers. Preparation for outdoor fieldwork can be the perfect opportunity to discuss current knowledge about the harmful effects of exposure to UV radiation from natural and artificial sources.

Hats, long-sleeved clothing, and sunblock are necessary precautions for everyone working in the outdoors. Be sure lips and ears are also protected. Cumulative UV exposure is also thought to be harmful to eyes, so UV-blocking sunglasses may also be in order.

Heat and dehydration are also factors to be considered. Make sure the work area does not get too hot—or too cold—and that everyone remembers to drink plenty of fluids.

SURE FOOTING

Sturdy protective footwear is a must at most field sites and for trips that involve substantial walking or hiking. But where you step is also important. Twisted ankles are frequently the consequence of slipping on what appears to be a solid surface. Warn all participants to be especially cautious of stepping on rocks or logs with dark-colored surfaces that may be moss or algae growth and treacherously slippery. Be equally aware that stones and boulders may come loose, and fallen branches and logs can roll. When standing in or wading through water, it may be difficult to discern whether the footing beneath is uneven or soft, so steps need to be careful and slow, with everyone testing the footing before putting down his or her full weight.

9

What's the Weather?

You may not be able to control the weather, but you better make sure you're prepared for it. Know what the variations in temperature and weather can be at the site you choose. What are the risks of sudden storms or flooding? Be sure you know, and make sure you have a shelter and evacuation plan.

Insist that your students be properly dressed for the weather. You may have students who come without gloves or hats. Simple gardening gloves or stocking hats might be a good extra provision. You are liable for making sure your students are dressed appropriately for all weather possibilities.

If you are planning a trip into the mountains, special consideration must be given to proper clothing. A generalization of mountaineers is that winter conditions may be encountered at any time when you are above 5,000 feet in elevation. During a midsummer trek to the heather meadows, you can encounter a sudden full winterlike storm. Be prepared. The old trappers and prospectors were not wearing wool clothing for the style. They knew that wool clothing retains its insulating properties even when wet.

Lightning is extremely dangerous. Many people are struck and killed by lightning each year. Even indoors, lightning can come through an open window or door and electrify a metal worktable. Instruct students to seek shelter if thunder is heard— at any distance. Once inside a shelter, do not use electrical equipment or work on metal structures. Don't take chances.

Flash flooding can also be life-threatening. You must check weather forecasts and escape routes immediately before entering any area where there is any potential for stranding.

Dangerous riptides can occur days before a storm appears or follow days after ocean storms occur miles away. Check regular forecasts, marine forecasts, and Coast Guard alerts.

Equipment and Supplies

When planning for an outdoor activity, you need to think about two categories of equipment and supplies:

▶ Items needed to complete the planned activities

▶ Items needed to promote group safety

You also need to make sure equipment used outdoors is sturdier and less breakable than what you might use in the more controlled environment of your classroom. Try to avoid anything made of glass and anything fragile or brittle—for instance, use plastic sampling containers rather than glass, metal probes rather than glass, and plastic hand lenses or field microscopes and water magnifiers rather than regular microscopes.

Weight and bulk should also be considered. Make student pairs or groups responsible for carrying and accounting for specific items, and then make sure the materials are packed for safe transport and are light enough for the students to handle easily. Plan sufficient time for equipment to be returned, counted, and repacked before leaving the field site.

Dress and footwear should not be left to chance or imagination. Make sure you provide students and parents with a clear list of appropriate clothing and shoes for the outdoor adventure. Dressing in layers is a useful strategy. It allows for adjustments to be made at the site. Hats are useful in both hot and cold situations. In sunny weather, they provide shade; in cold weather, they protect from loss of body heat. Shoes need to provide good support for the arches and ankles and have nonslip soles. Open-toed shoes, sandals, thongs, and slipper styles are inappropriate for fieldwork. Extra toe protection and waterproofing are highly desirable.

Communicate dress requirements clearly to parents, and offer help if a student does not own the appropriate clothing. Many students don't own shoes or hats of the type needed for fieldwork and others may not have the support at home to make sure they are ready, so, before the day of the trip, check all clothing and gear students are proposing to wear. Your school or class parent group may be able to assist students who have financial or other difficulty in obtaining appropriate dress and footwear for fieldwork.

What to include in your first aid kit depends upon the hazards of the site. Plan your first aid kit item by item rather than generically. Involve students in the preparation and selection of first aid supplies, and determine what first aid material each student should carry, and what should be carried for general purposes. Bring copies of all emergency medical information and permission slips along.

Make sure you have sufficient drinking water or other beverages for the duration of the trip. As a consequence, you will also need to plan for restroom availability. Be sure to bring trash bags to clean up your work areas and haul out trash. When you leave a study site, there should be no evidence that you were there. The next person or group to visit the area should find it at least as clean and unspoiled as when you arrived, if not better.

Be equally clear about items that should not be brought along, especially items that may add unnecessarily to the weight and bulk of transported materials and items that could dangerously distract students from educational tasks and safety precautions.

Overnights

High school teachers may wish to schedule extended overnight field experiences for students. These trips may be planned for regular classes, as special experiences open to students with prerequisite qualifications, or for clubs. The value of these experiences can be immeasurable, but there are also serious concerns that must be addressed by careful thought and planning. While the extensive preparation and precautions necessary for overnight trips are beyond the scope of this book, we include some points for you to consider.

The first thing you must do is to make a thorough study of your district's policies, insurance coverage, and the special needs of the students who might want to attend. As with other experiences, your trip should be made accessible to every academically qualified student, so you should find means to accommodate special needs and financial constraints. Fund-raising may be required to assist students who may need financial assistance but are otherwise fully qualified to participate.

To minimize disruption to your own and your colleagues' ongoing academic programs, consider scheduling overnight trips during weekends or school vacations. Also think carefully about how students and classes not included in the trip will be taught if you are not present. Loss of serious science instruction time due to substitute teachers who are not qualified to teach your program can place an unfair burden on students you leave behind during an extended field trip.

For transportation and facility arrangements, use a professional travel agent with credentials acceptable to school authorities and successful educational trip-planning experience.

The Seductiveness of Cell Phones

Cell phones—everyone, students and teachers alike, seems to have one—can become a dangerous substitute for caution and common sense. Remember this, cell phones depend on the existence of cells and transmission towers—no cell, no communication. Do not assume that cell phones will work in all locations. And never decide to go where you would otherwise not risk going just because you think you can call for help on your cell phone. For communications and check-in between groups and leaders, walkie-talkies set to the same channel may be more effective and reliable than cell phones. These also may not function in all terrains and should not substitute for keeping groups within close range of each other.

9

Making students and their parents stakeholders in the experience and setting clear rules with firm consequences are imperative. Establish the perimeter of travel, the rules of behavior, the curfews, and the consequences for substance abuse in conjunction with building administrators well in advance of formal announcement of the trip. Meet with parents and guardians to explain the rules, and let them know that violation of the rules will result in an immediate return for their student, at the parents' expense.

Include chaperones that are well-trained, firm, and used to working with teens. On extended field trips, you will need extra chaperones just for your own sanity. Someone will need to do the curfew bed check, the second check after curfew, the late night and the early morning shifts. You can't do it all. Bring sufficient trained help to avoid exhausting yourself.

Recognize that some high school students have never been away from their home or community overnight. Do not be surprised if some students suffer from homesickness or insomnia due to unfamiliar surroundings.

THE MONSTER

One of the most popular field trips for many science classes is an annual excursion to the regional amusement park. There are valuable lessons to be learned as the roller coaster plummets or the tilt-o-whirl spins. Thousands of students safely and securely make these trips each year. But there are accidents, too.

Before you even announce a possible trip to the amusement park, meet with park personnel. Many centers recommend specific days for students. On those days the entire park staff will be prepared for calculators, accelerometers, and complex questions. There will be someone in charge of education, and another person responsible for security. Meet with both. Find out the park's rules about smoking, and make sure that alcohol will not be available. Since many parks check backpacks at the gate, make sure your equipment is clearly marked and recognizable to the gate guards.

The amusement park is a place where you'll never be able to keep the class together, so structured groups are a must. Think of the park as a series of learning centers, and set up a schedule that students must follow to move through the stations.

9

Before the trip, take time to discuss the consequences of horseplay. There are serious dangers in amusement park rides, and your students must take them seriously. Let them know they must treat park staff respectfully and that they will be sent home immediately at their parents' expense for infractions of the rules.

Permissions

Your district or school may have a standard form permission slip. If so, you should begin with that document. However, because science field trips may entail more complexity than other field trips, make sure you include additional information that alerts parents and guardians to the nature of the activities planned and the special preparation, such as clothing requirements, that might have to be made. Request, too, that parents and guardians make you aware of special problems, such as allergies, their student may have even if they have already done so. For trips ending after the end of the school day, ask parents to be explicit about what arrangements they have made for their student upon return from the trip, including express permission from parents if students are to be permitted to leave the disembarkation point on their own.

Foreign Travel

For foreign travel, check U.S. State Department travel advisories at *travel.state.gov/travel_warnings. html.* Consult with hospital travel clinics and Centers for Disease Control (CDC) bulletins (online at *www.cdc.gov*) for immunization information.

The permission slip cannot relieve you or the school of liability for student safety. But it is an important legal document to show you were well organized and had planned carefully. Be sure to have the document(s) you use approved by your district's legal counsel.

Special Needs

Special needs students can and should be included in all planned field activities.

Many outdoor facilities are now equipped with ramps for wheelchair access, Braille trail signs for the sight impaired, and other modifications to promote accessibility. In some cases, teachers and students helped design and prepare these accommodations.

If you are going to a structured site such as a museum, nature center, or amusement park, make arrangements with the site's accessibility coordinator. If you are planning work at an informal or unimproved field site, work with support personnel, such as special education instructors and physical and occupational therapists, to ensure safe, maximum participation of special needs students.

9

SAMPLE HEALTH INFORMATION FORM

Source: *The Brookline Public Schools, Mass.*

For overnight, out-of-state, and out-of country field trips

Child's name _____ Date of Birth _____

Address _____ Telephone # _____

Parents/Guardians

Name _____ Work Phone # _____

Name _____ Work Phone # _____

Family Doctor _____ Telephone # _____

Emergency Contact Person (If parents/guardians not available)

Name _____ Phone # _____

Address _____ Work Phone # _____

HEALTH INFORMATION

1. Is there a PEANUT, BEE STING, or INSECT allergy?____If yes, treatment_____

_____

Any other allergies (food, aspirin, etc.)?____ What?_____ If yes, treatment _____

_____

2. Does your child have any medical condition?_____If yes, state diagnosis, treatment, medication _____

3. Has your child been exposed to any communicable diseases within the past 21 days? ____ If yes, specify _____

4. Is there any factor that makes it advisable for your child to follow a limited program of physical activity, i.e., heart, recent fracture or surgery, asthma, abnormal fear? _____ If yes, specify in which ways you wish his/her program limited.

_____

5. To protect your child from any possible embarrassment, does he/she wet at night?_____ sleep walk _____?

6. Please list date of the most recent tetanus shot _____

7. Is your child bringing medication, including over-the-counter and prescription? _____ If yes, complete the Medication Administration Form on the reverse side.

*Medications MUST be properly labeled in their original containers.

9

Parents/guardians will be contacted in case of serious sickness or accident. However, in the event of an emergency situation that requires immediate medical attention I, the parent (guardian), hereby give permission to the physician selected by the director or the trip leader in charge to hospitalize, secure proper treatment for, and to order injection, anesthesia, or surgery for my child as named above.

Signed: _____ Relationship: _____ Date: _____

SAMPLE MEDICATION ADMINISTRATION FORM

Each medication (including vitamins and supplements) must have a separate listing and complete instructions or the medication cannot be administered.

Child's name _____

1. (Medication) _____
(Dosage/How much) _____ (Frequency/How often) _____
(Diagnosis/Symptoms/What is this being administered for?) _____

_____

2. (Medication) _____
(Dosage/How much) _____ (Frequency/How often) _____
(Diagnosis/Symptoms/What is this being administered for?) _____

_____

3. (Medication) _____
(Dosage/How much) _____ (Frequency/How often) _____
(Diagnosis/Symptoms/What is this being administered for?) _____

_____

YES	NO	
_____	_____	My child may be given Tylenol.
_____	_____	My child may be given Benadryl.
_____	_____	My child may use insect repellent.
_____	_____	My child may use sunscreen.

Prescribed medication **must** be in a prescription bottle with a pharmacy label containing the child's name, the name of the medication, the dosage, and directions for administration. All nonprescription medication must be in the **original** container with directions for use, labeled with the child's name, and with a licensed prescriber's note.

Signed: _____ Relationship: _____ Date: _____

Take Nothing but Pictures, Leave Nothing but Footprints

If you concentrate on activities aimed at collecting data rather than specimens at field sites, you protect yourself as well as the environment. Before planning an activity that results in removing something from or irreversibly disturbing the field study area, ask yourself if there is any other reasonable way you can accomplish the same educational goals. Science is more about observing than about collecting, so the less intervention with the observed system the better. If you and your students can observe without touching, so much the better. Let the hands be on the instruments rather than on the organisms. That way, you minimize the hazards unknown or unanticipated organisms can pose and you make the fewest changes in the ecosystem you visit. You minimize contacts with potential allergens or infectious agents, and you avoid the inadvertent removal or harming of protected species.

Similarly, plan on carrying out everything you bring into a field site, including used materials, leftover supplies, and trash. Each outdoor environment has its own, delicately balanced, perhaps unique, ecosystem. For that reason, you should not simply release classroom-raised organisms to the outdoors. They may be completely alien species, unable to survive, or, worse, they may have insufficient predators. The introduction of an alien species can negatively alter an environment forever.

9

THE SAVVY SCIENCE TEACHER

Lincoln High School students love their lessons in amusement park physics. Their website presents their lessons, their experiences, and the cautionary advice they wish to share with other students.

When they trek, Lincoln students take a specially designed fanny pack that has been modified to fit the needs of park safety and still make it easy for students to collect data. Their CBLs (calculator-based laboratory) have had hook and loop strips added so that a Plexiglass shield can be placed over the LCD (liquid crystal display). Two holes were drilled in the shield so students can turn the instrument on without having to raise the shield.

Lincoln students are trained to use the equipment long before they hit the park. They practice activities at school, attaching instruments to pendulums, springs, cars on tracks, wheels, and turntables.

Check out their website at *lhs.lps.org/instruct/amuseweb/planning.htm* to understand how Lincoln High students rule the roller coaster.

Connections

▶ *Amusement park physics.* 1997–2003. Annnenberg/ CPB. See *www.learner. org/exhibits/park physics.*
▶ Robertson, W. C. 2001. *Community connections for science education: building successful partnerships.* Arlington, VA: NSTA Press. See *www.nsta.org/main/ pdfs/store/ PB160X1np.pdf* .
▶ Russell, H. R. 2001. *Ten- minute field trips.* Arlington, VA: NSTA Press.
▶ Kids' Lightning Information and Safety. See *www. azstarnet.com/anubis/ zaphome.htm.*
▶ Centers for Disease Control. See *www.cdc.gov/travel/ yb/index.htm.*
▶ Department of State. See *travel.state.gov/ travel_warnings.html.*

9

The Kitchen Sink
A Potpourri of Safety Tips

High school science teaching in the twenty-first century is considerably more complex than in the twentieth century. Research and discovery adds to the science knowledge base on a daily basis. With new information comes increased understanding of risks and steps that are needed to ensure safety. Although some safety issues are closely allied to a specific science subdiscipline, many issues, such as eye protection, arise in almost any science class or science discipline. This chapter contains the information most likely to be applicable in many different science disciplines and settings. In some cases, more details are provided for precautions mentioned briefly in earlier chapters.

Y ou may have found this book has touched on topics you never thought were the responsibility of a high school science teacher. Some issues may be new to you, for example your responsibility to ensure that students with special needs have every opportunity to acquire the same knowledge and skills as students without special needs—even if you must make special accommodations and modifications in your methods of teaching and assessment. But they are indeed very much your legal responsibility.

In other cases, you may not be primarily responsible, but an awareness of the issues and an understanding of appropriate decisions are a part of your responsibility. Our aim has been to be comprehensive, providing you with thorough information as well as information which you may need to share with building and district administrators.

Persistent Problems

Although it is relatively easy to analyze the safety concerns that might be related to a single lab activity, we sometimes take the general conditions of our assigned classroom spaces for granted. We now know some of the buildings we occupy are not as healthful an environment as they should be. Older structures may contain lead paint, asbestos insulation, or lead pipe. Asthma, allergies, and other persistent symptoms seem to be on the rise as buildings are made more airtight. Be alert to such signs as lingering coughs, sneezing, eye rubbing, headaches, and lethargy. They may be a signal that some irritant is present in your facility.

10

The Not-So-Magic Carpet

Carpets have never been recommended for laboratory classrooms. But many schools still have them, because, at some point in the past, administrators opted for sound reduction over safety. If the room you use for lab activities was converted from a regular classroom, there may even be wall-to-wall carpeting.

If possible, request the removal of all carpeting from science rooms. This floor covering may be the source of a host of problems difficult to trace or resolve. The substance most frequently used in science activities is water, both as a chemical reagent and for cleanup. A wet carpet makes an ideal breeding ground for the molds and mildew that are the most frequent and persistent cause of allergies and asthma in a closed environment. The glues and adhesives from newly installed carpet may outgas, causing mild but persistent headaches or dizziness. Infrequently or improperly cleaned carpets can harbor dust mites, dander, and other allergens and disease-causing organisms. Spilled fluids can penetrate to carpet backing and padding, so surfaces that appear clean may be covering contaminated material below. The highly recommended alternative to carpets is nonskid resilient flooring.

In some cases, it may not be possible to remove carpet right away. For example, in older schools, removing carpet might trigger the costly process of taking care of asbestos in floor tiles below. If problem carpeting cannot be removed, request a thorough cleaning with mildew treatment. Make sure the room is ventilated after treatment so the fluids can evaporate quickly. Even with thorough cleaning, some dander cannot be removed from carpets, so classroom pets, mammals in particular, should never be allowed on carpeted floors. The upholstery of old furniture may pose similar problems.

The Class Menagerie

If you have animals or many plants in your room, the food, waste, and soils can harbor mold and spores that last for years in the air of a classroom. Parasitic cysts from animal waste, classroom pets, and dissection specimens can resist all common cleaning agents. Limit the number of plants you keep, and use commercial potting soil. Do not bring animal carcasses into the classroom. (See Chapter 5, "Lively Science," p. 67.)

Heavy Metal Is More Than Loud Music

Heavy metal and organic compounds can persist in cracks and crevices in flooring and furniture despite regular cleaning. Curriculums have changed over the years. Many compounds once used for science activities and cleaning in years past are now known to be hazardous—toxic or carcinogenic. Mercury used in older thermometers and other measuring instruments poses the greatest hazard. Replace all mercury-filled instruments and turn over the old instruments for hazardous waste disposal. If you see traces of spilled mercury in your room, request hazardous waste removal services. Some states require immediate evacuation of the room or building until all spilled mercury has been removed.

Potable Water

Although most schools have municipal or well water that is tested and safe, some older schools have questionable sources or aging galvanized iron systems soldered with lead. If your school water is not certified as safe for drinking, make the issue and the reasons for it a science lesson for students. Prepare a proactive action plan to have adequate water supplied to the science area. Make sure your students know the nearest source of potable water, and identify it with signs and frequent reminders. In general, that shouldn't be in the laboratory room, but out in the hallway, so that the rule "No eating or drinking in the lab" can be enforced consistently.

Keeping Clean

The newest cleaning formulas increasingly tout their germ-killing ingredients. It is important to recognize just how many and what kinds of weapons need to be brought to the battle with germs. More often than not, just plain soap and warm water are enough. Sometimes a 10% solution of household bleach solution is all that is needed. Antibiotic hand cleaners are not recommended for daily use because science classes should not contribute to the selective evolution of super germs. Material safety data sheets (MSDS) are required for every product in your room. This includes all cleaning products. (For more information on MSDS, refer to Chapter 4, p. 52.)

In some cases, frequent soap-and-water hand washing by people with sensitive skin may result in chapping and skin breaks, which can cause problems of their own. Try substituting hand-cleaning gels made of quick-drying alcohol formulations, keeping in mind their flammability. Another solution is using disposable gloves. Model the surgeon's technique of removing disposable gloves by flipping them inside out.

Hepatitis

> Hepatitis A is a liver disease spread by bad hygiene and contaminated food.

> Hepatitis B is a viral liver disease spread by body fluids, including saliva and blood. It can be spread by biting and spitting. It is often chronic.

> Hepatitis C is a viral liver disease spread by body fluids. It is the least-known form and often lies dormant for many years before causing serious symptoms and sometimes death.

Recent changes in federal and some state laws require that schools restrict the amount and types of materials used for cleaning, disinfecting, and pest control. In some cases, parents and others must be notified before certain chemicals are applied. Check to be sure you are not using some cleaning agent or disinfectant material that is banned or restricted from use in school buildings. Use the information on the MSDS, and check with building administrators and school facilities personnel. A good rule: Use the mildest possible chemical to perform the task.

10

Standard (Universal) Precautions— Typical School Practices

▶ Never bring blood or blood products into the classroom.

▶ Always have nonlatex gloves available for use in cases of bleeding.

▶ Provide sterile gauze pads to the injured individual to cover and hold over the wound.

▶ Do not interfere in a fight in a manner that could expose you to blood or biting.

▶ Use approved disinfectants for blood or body fluid spills. To prevent splashing and further contamination, cover the spill with paper towels or absorbent cloth such as an old T-shirt, then pour the disinfectant over the towels or cloth. Use a specially marked disposal container for all materials contaminated with blood and other body fluids.

▶ All designated personnel who might be asked to clean up body fluids such as blood, saliva, or vomitus should be vaccinated against hepatitis B.

▶ Have a special waste container for biohazards. Refer to your school and community health services for specifics.

First Aid

It's reasonable and prudent to be prepared for the unexpected. First aid training courses from the American Red Cross are highly recommended. Most states have Good Samaritan laws that provide liability protection for a trained emergency response. Check to find the specifics in your state.

For a person with a severe allergy, an EpiPen or adrenalin injection can be of critical importance and is easily administered by a properly trained person. Without it, anaphylactic shock from an insect sting could result in a fatality. Although relatively simple to use, it must be administered only by prescription by a nurse or person trained by the prescribing physician. Find out about your district policy, and make sure you or someone else is trained to use an EpiPen. This is especially important on field trips.

Standard (Universal) Precautions

In response to possible hazards associated with bloodborne pathogens, the United States Occupational Safety and Health Administration (OSHA) required the use of Universal Precautions for the handling of human blood. When it was recognized that other body fluids might also carry and transmit pathogens, these practices were later expanded to include the handling of any human body fluids and are now called Standard Precautions

The handling of body fluids such as blood, saliva, and vomitus requires prior training in the proper procedures to protect against transmission of pathogens such as human immunodeficiency virus (HIV) and hepatitis. Hepatitis vaccination is normally recommended if you have these responsibilities. The accepted standard of care is to use Standard Precautions in all instances involving body fluids. Check with your school

10

health officer for specifics on how the Standard Precautions are implemented in your district. The body fluids from any person should be treated as if they might be infectious—no exceptions. All school personnel should have refresher training every year.

Use and Disposal of Sharps

Sharps include tools, parts of tools, and broken objects with sharp edges or points that can break the skin and cause cuts or other injuries. Metal blades, needles, broken glass, and plastic with jagged edges are all considered sharps. If you use materials that have sharp points or edges or that can be broken into pieces with points or sharp edges, you must prepare a separate disposal container for them. This container should not be opened or emptied, but rather disposed of intact and then replaced with a new one. Make sure everyone who uses your room or handles your trash knows about the sharps container, uses it, and handles it correctly.

You and your students can easily make sharps disposal containers. You can use a plastic gallon jug or a corrugated box sealed on all sides. Cut a small slot in the container large enough to accept broken or sharp items for disposal. Label the sharps disposal container prominently on all sides—color it red or place a red label on it. Make sure your custodian will recognize it immediately. If an object with sharp or broken edges is too large for your regular sharps container, make a special one just for that object. Keep one or two small cardboard boxes just for this purpose. Be sure to seal and label it clearly, and place it near the regular sharps container for disposal.

Sharp and pointed instruments can be very tempting for students. So carefully inventory all sharp items distributed for use during class. Take a tip from the shop teacher and try organizing the placement of the various instruments so that missing items are easily spotted. Another method is to color-code each group's instruments with nail polish, permanent markers, or paint to make an easily seen visual pattern such as a diagonal stripe that highlights missing items.

If someone does get cut, be sure to observe Standard Precautions for handling body fluids in treating the blood and wound.

The Latex Connection

Latex has been identified as a serious allergen—causing reactions as simple as rash and irritation and as serious as anaphylactic shock. Common sources of latex in the classroom are in "rubber" gloves, both disposable and nondisposable. Nonlatex (e.g., nitrile) gloves are recommended instead of latex gloves. Rubber tubing, rubber dams, and some flexible connectors may also be made of latex.

10

Another source of latex in the classroom is the common balloon. In addition to their allergenic potential, these balloons present a choking hazard if students fool around while blowing them up.

Red Means Stop, Green Means Go—Or Do They?

Color blindness, particularly red-green color blindness, is more common than most people suspect. If you use color-coding in organizing your room or activities, particularly if you use red to symbolize a safety warning or precaution, make sure you also include verbal or graphic indicators so color-blind individuals do not miss your meaning or distinction. This sex-linked trait, most often appearing in males, often goes unnoticed even into adulthood until some comic or unfortunate incident makes the effect apparent. It is highly unlikely any boys in your high school classes realize they are color-blind, even though some may be affected from mildly to severely.

Old Classics

The possibility of disease transmission through body fluids means the loss of some long-cherished lab activities such as the traditional cheek cell lab. Saliva is a body fluid. The classic cracker-chewing labs to demonstrate enzyme action on starch should not be used both because saliva is a body fluid and because nothing in the lab should be placed in the mouth, chewed, or eaten.

The Scientific Gourmet

There are many suggestions for edible science activities in books and curriculum resources. Investigations with food and cooking have long been a part of science activities, but these investigations present special problems.

No Cooking, Tasting, or Eating

There should be no eating or tasting in a science facility. The hidden dangers that come with consumption of food or drink in a science room or science activity fall into two categories. First, the area may be contaminated with surprisingly persistent toxins, including heavy metals, organic compounds, molds, and pathogens. In a shared science space, you can never be sure of what materials were there before or how well the space was cleaned. Second, students who are in the habit of eating in a science workspace may be tempted to taste a material that is meant for research. The best rule is the most simple: Nothing should be tasted or eaten as part of science lab work. No snacks or food should be eaten in a science room or in the part of the general room where investigations have taken place. This policy is consistent with regulatory requirements in research laboratories. The presence or consumption of food in a laboratory can result in a shutdown of the entire operation.

10

But what about those motivating experiences that involve foods, such as observing changes in popping corn or measuring the calories in croutons? There is no problem in using edible material in lab activities as long as none of it is consumed. Popcorn or croutons may be perfectly edible in cafeterias, theaters, and homes but not in a science lab.

Nut Allergies

An increasing number of students and adults have been identified with serious—often life-threatening—allergies to nuts. An allergic reaction may be triggered not only by ingestion but also by proximity to a nut or nut product. If such an allergic individual is present in your class, you must avoid investigations involving nuts, nut oils, and nut by products. School authorities may also have to take steps to eliminate these products in breakfast and lunch programs and provide separated eating facilities to ensure there is no exposure from snacks or other foods brought into the classroom or school building. Eliminating peanuts and peanut products from classrooms altogether would be prudent. Use croutons instead of peanuts for the traditional calorie laboratory. Confer with the school nurse to get information on student allergies at the beginning of the year.

Dress of the Day

Dress codes may be controversial in the school in general, but in the science classroom, safety takes precedence. Some clothing fashions are just poor choices for science activities. It is both legal and practical to set a commonsense dress code in your science classroom.

Begin with the philosophy that the classroom is a "workplace"—an environment where commonsense clothing is required. Loosely hanging, floppy clothing and hanging jewelry are not reasonable. If a student insists a particular piece of jewelry cannot be removed, cover it completely with tape or a bandage.

10

Combustible Fabrics

Even when you've controlled for the major fashion crazes, you may still have trouble with the fabrics in student clothing. Many are highly flammable and may also melt at relatively low temperatures, causing severe burns and permanent injuries. Ask for help from your local fire department to demonstrate the high flammability of fabrics, especially filmy, gauzy fabrics. Teach students what to do if clothing catches fire—stop, drop, and roll. It may be relevant and motivating to have students test flammability of a variety of fabrics found in contemporary clothing and bedding and draw their own conclusions with respect to risk.

Coats, jackets, hats, and similar loose-fitting, over-hanging, and dangling articles should be removed and stored away from work and lab areas. Bare midriffs are not acceptable. Absorbent watchbands and wrist ornaments should be removed. Hair should be tied, pinned, or otherwise secured back behind the shoulders. Backpacks and totes should be stored in lockers or other storage areas. Shoes should have closed toes and be securely tied. No platform shoes or any other footwear that is likely to result in tripping and falling should be worn in a science laboratory. This is a matter of safe practice rather than fashion commentary. And of course, remind the adults (especially aides, interns, and student teachers) to conform to the same dress guidelines. Provide a copy of your dress code to the administration and your district's legal counsel to make sure you have agreement and support for the consequences that you will impose if the dress code is not followed. Following this vetting process, provide copies to all students and parents.

All Eyes on Science

Clear vision and protection of the eyes is a must in almost any laboratory activity.

Contact Lenses

Contact lens technology has made possible excellent correction of many severe vision conditions. In many cases, contact lenses may afford better vision than regular eyeglasses. Contact lenses can be worn with well-fitting safety glasses if there is no risk of exposure to fumes. However, contact lenses, especially soft contact lenses, may absorb chemical fumes or otherwise trap chemicals in the eye, rendering eyewash ineffective. They should not be worn, with or without safety glasses, if there is a risk of exposure to strong chemical fumes. But if you run into a lab with that potential risk, it makes good sense to ask "Should this lab activity be done in my class at all?" Lungs are as sensitive as eyes—you should be avoiding the fumes.

Eye Protection

Many teachers associate eye protection with chemistry activities, but it is also a must in many other circumstances. There are two primary kinds of eye protection devices: safety glasses and safety goggles. All devices need to comply with the

10

requirement of the ANSI Z87.1 standard, a voluntary standard of the safety industry and required by the Occupational Safety and Health Administration (OSHA).

Safety glasses have side shields and are intended to protect against minor impact hazards. Goggles are designed to surround the eyes and fit the faces snugly.

There are two major types of safety goggles. Safety goggles can be designed for chemical splash protection and/or impact protection. Impact goggles are directly vented and appropriate for more serious impact situations such as projectiles in physics or in a woodworking shop.

Chemical splash goggles are indirectly vented. Chemical splash goggles should be worn whenever a chemical or hot liquid hazard is present. Chemical splash goggles that are ANSI Z87.1-compliant will also provide proper protection for impact hazards. **ANSI Z87.1-compliant chemical splash goggles are the type of goggles that we strongly recommend you use exclusively.** (All ANSI Z87.1-compliant chemical splash goggles are also impact-resistant.)

Neither safety glasses nor safety goggles are intended to protect the rest of your face and your throat. In some instances, a face shield may be necessary to use for that purpose, in addition to either safety glasses or safety goggles. They are often used in college laboratories, and teachers may need them when they prepare dilutions and solutions. But we strongly urge that you reconsider any secondary level experiment that would require the use of face shields. It would be better for high school students to use smaller quantities, different reagents, or simulations. We do not recommend any secondary student activity that is so dangerous that a face shield is required.

Any activity that can generate projectiles requires either safety spectacles with side shields or safety goggles (depending on the severity of the impact). They should be marked ANSI Z87.1.

Conjunctivitis

Conjunctivitis (sometimes called pinkeye) is highly contagious and can easily be spread from one user to another via contamination of safety eyewear and optical instruments such as microscopes, binoculars, and telescopes. Decontamination and disinfection of shared-use safety eyewear is a must. For optical instruments, this may be more difficult. Remind students that, to use a microscope properly, you do not need to touch your eye to the eyepiece. We also recommend use of removable eye guards that can be cleaned with warm soapy water or alcohol between uses. Harsh cleaning solutions or alcohol applied to optical instrument lenses may permanently damage the lenses and lens coatings, so check manufacturer's care guides and follow instructions carefully. The school nurse may need to check students with red and itchy eyes, since conjunctivitis is an infectious disease that may warrant exclusion from school until the student is no longer contagious.

10

Any activity that involves use of any chemical (in liquid, solid, or powder form) which could injure the eye—including dissection activities—requires splashproof eye protection. Chemical splash goggles often have baffles that permit air to circulate without allowing harmful chemicals to directly enter. Students sometimes remove or flip open the baffles. Be sure to warn against that practice and insist that baffles be in proper position.

Regular eyeglasses or plastic spectacles (also called "plant visitor specs") are not acceptable substitutes for ANSI Z87.1-compliant eye protection.

Try using a sign: "Welcome—It's an Eye Protection Day," to signal students as they enter the lab. Even with the use of eye protection, always have the eyewash flushed clean and ready to use. (See Chapter 3, p. 33, for more information on eyewashes.)

Disinfecting Safety Eyewear

If safety goggles are shared, they must be sterilized after every use, either in an ultraviolet (UV) cabinet or in hot water and detergent or disinfectant, to prevent the spread of conjunctivitis and hepatitis. UV cabinets are not as high-tech as they seem. If goggles are just tossed haphazardly into them, the light sometimes doesn't reach all the surfaces and disinfection is unreliable.

A simpler procedure is for departing students to drop their goggles into a sink filled with antibacterial dishwashing solution. Entering students can thoroughly rinse and dry the goggles and wear them immediately afterward. If you use this method, make sure straps are plastic rather than cloth. Have plenty of soft clean towels available, because rough paper towels can scratch the plastic lenses.

Yet another alternative is to have a personal pair of safety goggles for each student and instructor with just a few extra pairs available for use by visitors. If students are issued or purchase combination chemical splash and impact-resistant safety goggles upon entry to high school and care for them appropriately, the goggles can last through all high school science classes (and perhaps jewelry-making and shop classes as well). Replacement lenses, baffles, and straps are available for most high-quality safety goggles.

Pregnancies

Although we hate to face the possibility, high school girls become pregnant. Take note of signs of illness and refer any student with possible problems to the proper school counseling or nursing staff. In science, some chemicals—such as some biological stains and preservatives and many solvents and organic compounds—are teratogens and pose serious risk to the fetuses of pregnant women. Since you may not know if a student or colleague is pregnant, the best thing to do is to avoid completely the use of teratogenic chemicals.

It Seemed Great When I Did It...	A Better High School Alternative
Dissecting preserved specimens	Examining muscles, bones, and cartilage in chicken wings or dissect squid and fish in a sanitary way
Acid-base titration experiments	pH changes in aging soda pop
Phenolphthalein indicator for pH	Cabbage juice, beet juice, or tea as indicators of pH
Generation and testing of hydrogen	Investigating carbon dioxide generated by an antacid tablet
Violent exothermic chemical reactions	Heat of vaporization lab—a.k.a. watching water boil
Culturing environmental bacteria	Culturing yeast, surveying water for plankton to monitor water quality
Van de Graaff generators	Batteries and bulbs
Measuring the respiration of lab animals	Measuring the respiration of *Elodea*
Testing pond water with strong reagents	Testing pond water with probeware
Tasting phenylthiocarbamide (PTC) paper to test for a gene	Checking tongue-rolling ability to test for a gene
Killing insects with chloroform for collections	Field observations of insects
Chromatography requiring petroleum ether	Chromatography using water-soluble samples such as nonpermanent markers

The Internet Connection

The National Science Education Standards (NRC 1996) encourage teachers to go beyond the walls of their classrooms, taking students both virtually and physically into contact with real science. The Internet provides many opportunities, but sites must be screened carefully for accuracy and usefulness. Create a hot list or website where your students can link to specific sites. Remember you are responsible for ensuring your students' work on the Internet is carefully designed and supervised to keep them as safe as possible when they venture into this learning environment.

10

Unlike formal print publications, the information posted on Internet websites need not be edited or vetted. False, misleading, and downright dangerous information is just as prevalent on the Internet as accurate, up-to-date, and useful information. It is therefore essential that you provide students with carefully structured Internet assignments and that you have screened all the sites you direct them to use.

Unsupervised exploration is an invitation to disaster. Although most schools have Internet filters in place to comply with federal law, it is important to understand that these filters are not foolproof. Translation: In many instances, they simply don't work. So make sure your students have clear, timed assignments. Arrange the monitors so an adult supervisor can see them at all times, and circulate around the room to view all the screens frequently. Check student interactions to make sure they are on task.

Pornographers, pedophiles, hate groups, anarchists, and members of cults and fringe groups use the Internet to contact young people. Some software may help deter students from identifying themselves online, but these electronic shields can be circumvented intentionally or unintentionally. Under no circumstances should students be allowed to provide their full names or demographic information on the Internet. E-mails to student pen pals should be screened through the teacher, using first names or pseudonyms. If you share group pictures of experiments or discoveries on the Internet, identify them by classroom, not by student names. Never put identifiable pictures of students on the Internet.

Students should not be permitted to visit chat rooms except through certified educational programs. For example, both the National Science Teachers Association, found at *www.nsta.org*, and the JASON program, found at *www.jason.org*, offer well-supervised chats with researchers.

If your district has developed an Internet-use policy and a written contract to be signed by students and parents, be sure you know the policy and follow it carefully. The sample provided is a starting point, but, as with all the samples forms in this book, you should develop one that is aligned with local and state policy and approved by your district's legal counsel.

Independent Studies

Project-based learning and laboratory investigations sometimes allow students to shine who have not done so in traditional settings.

For some of these students, independent studies at the high school level can be valuable add-ons or can constitute an entire course of study. But advanced and independent projects may raise safety problems even more than remedial work. By design, such studies may have students investigating questions with as yet unknown answers. You must take special care to become familiar with chemicals and techniques that will be used.

SAMPLE INTERNET-USE GUIDELINES AND CONTRACT

Source: The Brookline Public Schools, Mass.

GUIDELINES

The primary purpose of the Internet connection is educational; therefore, the_____ School(s)

- ▶ *Takes no responsibility for any information or materials that are transferred through the Internet and requires users to refrain from downloading inappropriate, non-educational material;*

- ▶ *Will not be liable for the actions of anyone connecting to the Internet through this hook-up. All users shall assume full liability, legal, financial, or otherwise, for their actions;*

- ▶ *Makes no guarantees, implied or otherwise, regarding the reliability of the data connection. The _____ Schools shall not be liable for any loss or corruption of data resulting from use of the Internet connection;*

- ▶ *Reserves the right to examine all data stored in computers or on disks which are the property of the _____ Schools to ensure that users are in compliance with these regulations;*

- ▶ *Strongly condemns the illegal acquisition and/or distribution of software, otherwise known as pirating. Any users transferring such files through the Internet, and any whose accounts are found to contain such illegal files, may have their accounts permanently revoked;*

- ▶ *Reminds all users that when they use the Internet, they are entering a global community, and any actions taken by them will reflect upon the school system as a whole. As such, we expect that all users will behave in an ethical and legal manner;*

- ▶ *Reserves the right to change or modify these rules at any time without notice.*

Even though we refer to these studies as "independent work," it is not truly independent—of teacher responsibility, guidance, and oversight. You are liable for accidents, disposal, and safety standards even if you are not providing all the directions for that independent project.

One key to a safe independent project is to have thorough, written procedure documents. Demand that your students research every aspect of their proposed projects and create their own safety documents in great detail.

10

CONTRACT

I, _____, agree:

To abide by all rules which are listed in the _____ Schools Guidelines for Internet Use;

That the primary purpose of the _____ Schools Internet connection is educational;

That the use of the Internet is a privilege, not a right;

Not to participate in the transfer of inappropriate or illegal materials, including the intellectual property of others through the _____ Schools Internet connection;

Not to allow other individuals to use my account for Internet activities, nor will I give anyone my password.

I understand that inappropriate behavior may lead to penalties, which may include discipline, revocation of account, or legal action.

I realize that there are inappropriate and possibly offensive materials available to those who use the Internet, and the undersigned hereby releases the _____ Schools from any liability or damages that may result from the viewing of, or contact with, such materials.

Signed:_____ Date:_____

Parents must sign if the user is under eighteen years of age.

I, _____, the parent/guardian of the above, agree to accept all financial and legal liabilities which may result from my son's/daughter's use of the _____ Schools Internet connection.

Signed:_____ Date:_____

MY INTERNET CONTRACT

I, _____, promise to obey all school policies and rules about the Internet. I will only use search engines for appropriate school assignments. I will avoid inappropriate sites. I will not join chat rooms or use a personal e-mail account at school. I will not download material or change the settings on school computers. I understand that violation of these rules may result in discipline and loss of all computer privileges.

_____(Student)   _____(Parents)

10

If students work under your supervision, they must be in your sight. A stockroom is never a good place to work, and students do not belong there. Prep rooms are also poor choices for students working independently. The best choices are regular laboratory spaces that you can view and monitor at all times while the student is at work.

Even if you know where and how they will be used, never release chemicals for use outside your classroom and away from your supervision. Chemicals belong in your lab or in a university or commercial lab that meets the highest safety standards. You don't know how much security and safety equipment any other place would have. Always consider the worst-case scenarios—what could happen if all of the reagent were used inappropriately or if all of the reagent were ingested by an infant?

Independent study students often work with university or industrial mentors. But without prior conference and agreement with you, the standards these mentors apply may not be suitable for the maturity of your students. It may have been many years since the mentors were in high school. Their understanding of students may be based on their own high school experiences when safety standards were far laxer than today. Adults who work only occasionally with young people doing advanced work tend to think of the students as adults with the same level of reasoning and understanding as themselves.

Have an explicit discussion with mentors about the differences between high school and college skill levels, and document that you have done so. Specifically remind any others who may be working with independent students that the students are adolescents who will need understanding, guidance, and direct supervision at all times. While they may be good kids, they are first and foremost kids.

Make sure you give your independent study student's parents enough detail about the independent work that the parents can partner with you to ensure that the project does not stray from agreed-upon safety measures. Let parents know you are concerned about the safety of every independent project and that, if they have any questions, doubts, or uneasiness about what their child is doing, you should be contacted immediately.

Picture This

Public schools are required to protect a student's privacy rights. One area that often becomes an issue is photographing them.

At the beginning of each year, make sure district-approved parental consent documents have been obtained and filed before any photographs are taken. Before releasing any photographs to an outside entity, make sure you have the clear written consent of the parent or guardian and that you are following district rules.

Special circumstances may make even standard photo releases inappropriate. Students are sometimes the subjects of custody disputes, and photos can endanger their safety. Photos of disabled students and students in special needs classrooms might inadvertently subject a child to unwanted public attention. Photos of students in certain disciplinary or instructional situations might imply some negative connotations. When in doubt, ask the parents for written approval of the specific circumstance.

Privacy vs. Public Access

Your students and their parents have a reasonable expectation of privacy while students are in your care. They rely on your judgment. Reporters, researchers, and even police agency representatives do not have the right to question students without parental consent. One major exception: In almost every state, representatives of agencies responsible for child protective services and prevention of child abuse may question students in the presence of a school official without the permission of their parents.

Some of the most difficult privacy issues arise with divorced and separated parents whose rights depend on specific arrangements ordered by the courts. One of the key goals of effective schools is to be welcoming to parents and to their participation in their children's education. But in cases where noncustodial parents are barred by court order from contact with their children or participation in decisions concerning their children, the schools, and you as an employee, must comply. As a teacher, you may be directly approached by parents whose access to their children has been restricted by the courts. Your school administrator should advise you of district policy and precautions you must take regarding visits from noncustodial parents.

Many schools allow students to produce newspapers and videos for cable channels. When a regular student news or weather program is produced, you may be able to provide parents with a blanket permission slip for participation. If a special topic is planned, parents should again be asked for consent. This includes assignments where students are creating videos for science projects.

10

SAMPLE CONSENT AND RELEASE FORM

Source: The Brookline Public Schools, Mass.

Dear Parents:

We are often approached by reporters from newspapers, magazines, and television to interview, photograph, and/or videotape our students. These members of the press are often motivated to make these requests because of the nature of our instructional programs. Occasionally they will simply want a picture of children coming to school on the opening day. In addition, we may have textbook companies request that they be able to photograph a classroom at work to include in a recent publication.

We do not allow any children to be interviewed/photographed, and/or videotaped by the media and/or school personnel for publicity or newspapers without having your permission. I am asking that you indicate below whether you are willing to grant such permission. Please complete the tear-off and return it to your child's classroom teacher. Thank you for your assistance.

(Signature) _____

CONSENT AND RELEASE

I hereby grant [ ] or withhold [ ] permission for photographs, videotaping, and/or interviews of my child _____ to be used in school publications and/or outside media during the time she/he attends the _____ schools.

Parent/guardian signature:_____

Address:_____

Date:_____
(Reprinted with permission by the Brookline Public Schools.)

10

E.T. Phone Home— or E-Mail

Teachers need telephones and e-mail capability in their classrooms for ordinary communications as well as for emergencies. Parents need to be partners in your work with their children, and communication is critical to this partnership. The better teachers and parents know each other, the better they can work together to support students and ensure their safety at home and at school. At the very least, you need a functioning means of calling for help or reporting a problem instantly. Keep a log of your calls and other communications to document your ongoing efforts to keep everyone informed.

On the other hand, students don't need to be in contact with their friends every minute of every day. Cell phones are not only a distraction, but they can also be a security risk. Some states prohibit students from carrying cell phones in high schools. Even when cell phones are legal in school, they need to be powered off and put away during class time.

Crisis Prevention and Response

As the all-too-common headlines of school violence and crises show, this book could never describe everything needed for security. The most effective safety factor in a school is the staff. A caring, watchful group of adults can spot potential problems before they are even imagined.

Although organizing a large high school into smaller houses may cause problems in locating science classrooms and storerooms, there are offsetting benefits. Smaller groupings within a large physical facility may enhance the ability of faculty to be more familiar with individual students and give students more chance for personal attention. Regardless of the organization of your high school, you may still find time to mentor individual students.

Science teachers in particular can play key roles in crisis prevention. You have many opportunities to work with students in informal settings. When your students are engaged in lab activities in small groups or pairs, you have a good opportunity to observe and hear students' attitudes emerge. Put up your antennae for signs of troubled students. Report your observations to administrators and counselors. Follow up in writing. Never ignore threats or warning signs from students, assuming they are just kidding.

Additionally, keep outside doors closed, and make sure the students who enter your room are those enrolled in your class. Don't allow friends to enter, or students to stray away from the class. If you spot an intruder (student or unidentified adult) notify the school security staff at once.

Keep your room well organized and clutter-free. That way you are more likely to be aware of items that have been removed from your room or unusual items or bags

10

left there. Items you cannot identify as harmless should be reported and not handled. Do not ask students to bring large collections of items or unusually complex materials from home. This adds to clutter and ambiguity.

Keep your room locked when you aren't present. This is a challenge, especially during all-too-short changes of class. But you may be held liable for what happens in your classroom when you are not there.

Plan for the worst so you can securely enjoy the best of times. With your fellow staff members and the support of the administration, create and train crisis response teams to respond to medical and psychological crises, threats and acts of violence, and the range of circumstances that require immediate action for the welfare and safety of students and others in the schools. Such teams should plan for emergencies and ensure that individuals are trained and available to provide first aid, psychological support, physical security, and public information. Include and maintain regular contact with representatives from state and local agencies that provide assistance and emergency response—police and fire departments, community mental health agencies, local hospitals, state health departments.

> ## Promises to Keep
>
> Provide opportunities for informal conversation with your students, but do not promise secrecy. You need to assure students you will respect their private communications with you but not at the expense of failing to exercise your judgment in protecting them and others.

Planning for the Future

Don't wait until September to make plans for the coming year. When your principal begins to discuss next year's assignments, schedule an appointment to consider these priorities:

▶ *Class size*: Although additional facilities and equipment can make science safer for larger groups of students, the number of students that can be effectively and safely taught in an active investigative science program has a limit. There is a very high, positive correlation between class size and accident rate no matter how good the facilities. Although experts disagree on an absolute limit, statistics show accidents increase dramatically as classes increase beyond 20 to 24 students.

▶ *Scheduling:* Preparing for science activities takes thought and time. Equipment must be inventoried and checked for correct and safe functioning. Surfaces must be cleaned before and after messy activities. This kind of preparation cannot be done during a five-minute break or while students are doing seatwork. Preparation time needs to be scheduled rather than squeezed in, especially if you are team teaching, need to share space, or move from one location to another. Request firmly that you have similar classes scheduled in sequence, with a prep period between major subject changes.

10

- *Security:* In some states, two exits are required for science rooms. If your state does not require two exits for a science classroom, request a room with two exit doors that is not in a heavy-traffic area or near a major school entrance. Check for good communication with the office. Get a phone, and make sure it works. If you suspect old copies of your classroom key are floating around, ask for your room to be re-keyed. Keys to science storage areas and rooms solely dedicated to science instruction should be unique. These rooms should not be accessible with keys used to enter regular classrooms or common areas.

- *Physical Plant:* This is a good time to look to your surroundings and develop a positive action plan. What changes or repairs need to be made to the science area? Is there some modernization that would be a benefit to teaching science? What are your long-term goals? Does the ventilation system need overhaul and up-grading? Do you need additional secure storage areas with air vented directly to the outside? Do the eyewash stations supply clean and tepid water? Are there older glass-faced cabinets you would like removed from the teaching area? Now is the time to develop that plan, to work with the administration and establish a timeline to make the changes you would like to provide a better learning environment for the students. Remember that many of these changes may require ear-marking future funds and taking time to plan and complete. If your facilities requests are scheduled for several years hence, make sure they do not get dropped off the next versions of multiyear capital improvement plans.

Leave No Child Untested

At the national, state, and local levels, the pressure to demonstrate student achievement through tests has increased. The federal No Child Left Behind Act (NCLBA) of 2001 has increased the time, effort, and funding allocated to assessment at every level and placed additional emphasis on state-mandated, high-stakes graduation tests by placing sanctions on schools in which fewer than the mandated numbers of students pass the tests.

Most of the tests use an objective format because they are easier to develop and standardize (multiple-choice items) than open-ended items which test for analytic ability or laboratory technique.

The emphasis on testing makes many teachers feel there is little time left for laboratory investigations and for building safety skills in advance of laboratory investigations. If we skew our curriculum toward these tests, we may disenfranchise the curious, the gifted, or the student with nonverbal learning styles. But this needn't be the case. Research has demonstrated that students who are encouraged to investigate responsibly do better on all sorts of assessments. Logical reasoning skills extend to many contexts. Teaching students to observe carefully, follow directions, and think through their choices will make them not only safer investigators but better test takers as well.

10

It is important to assess safety skills authentically, not just at the start of the year but with every lesson. Although we can't provide a complete manual of ideas for authentic assessment in safety education, consider these:

▶ Safety requires specific skills at the outset. Before beginning a lesson, students may need to master accurate use of pipettes, Bunsen burners, or balances. Provide rubrics that permit students to self-assess or assess each other within a group. Build lessons in a way that requires students to master techniques and safe practices to the satisfaction of themselves and their peers before proceeding with the rest of the investigation.

▶ Require students to embed safety precautions into every lab report and portfolio presentation. Precautions that students themselves develop can be especially effective.

▶ Use safety scenarios as stems of multiple-choice items. Use a digital camera to photograph different setups. ("What problem do you see here?") Or describe the effects of improper equipment usage in a short paragraph. Students should be able to recognize not only the precautions they should take but also the results of poor techniques.

▶ Use news clips or stories of real-life accidents to prompt students to demonstrate their authentic understanding of good safety techniques.

After you use an assessment to identify a deficiency, then act. Develop a remediation lesson, an alternative method of helping students master the material, or a new lesson plan.

NCLBA and Teacher Qualification

NCLBA isn't just testing legislation. It contains some specific requirements for professional development. NCLBA now requires local education agencies to report the state certification and training status of all teachers it employs and the number of classes that are taught by teachers not appropriately certified and "highly qualified" to teach the subject and to make this information available to the public. "Highly qualified" and certification are left to the individual states to define. By the end of the 2005–6 academic year, in order to receive federal funding, school districts must ensure that all their teachers are certified and deemed "highly qualified" in any core academic course that they teach. The sciences are core academic courses. "Highly qualified" should include preparation for safety, but whether it does or not depends on the state. To access funding for your continued professional development, safety education will have to be built into your state and local NCLBA plan. So advocate for the help you need.

10

THE SAVVY SCIENCE TEACHER

Ms. F has taken a classic laboratory exercise a step farther. Once a year, she prepares a simple 4-oz. paper cup for each of her students. Most of them are half filled with clear water, but two from each class are "seeded" with baking soda.

When Ms. F distributes her cups, she solemnly warns her students they may not drink the liquid. But they may "share" fluids with up to three other students in the class, recording their exchanges carefully.

After about twenty minutes of "fluid exchanges," Ms. F asks all the students to present their cups. They will now be tested for a potential communicable disease. Into each cup she places a few drops of phenolphthalein. Those that turn pink are "infected."

Now Ms. F's students become disease detectives. Each infected student's name is placed on the board. The students are interviewed, and must report every person with whom they've "exchanged fluids." Their assessment is a report on how the condition was passed among the class community.

Ms. F has noticed her students seem less likely to be caught in lip-locks or sharing their drinks in the hall after her lab. She hopes that caution extends to the times when they can't be observed, as well.

Connections

▶ American Chemical Society and ACS Board–Council Committee on Chemical Safety. 2001. *Chemical safety for teachers and their supervisors.* Washington, DC: ACS. Available in PDF format at *membership. acs.org/c/ccs/pubs/ chemical_safety_ manual.pdf.*

▶ American Red Cross. 2001. *American Red Cross first aid: Responding to emergencies.* San Bruno, CA: Staywell.

▶ American Red Cross. 1992. *The American Red Cross first aid safety handbook.* Boston: Little Brown & Co.

▶ American Red Cross. 2002. *Community first aid safety.* San Bruno, CA: Staywell.

▶ Centers for Disease Control. See *www.cdc.gov/niosh.*

▶ National Institute for Occupational Safety and Health. See *www.cdc.gov/niosh.*

▶ NCLBA, The No Child Left Behind Act. See *www. ed.gov/nclb/ landing.jhtml.*

▶ Occupational Safety and Health Administration. See *www.osha. gov.*

▶ Waugh, M. 2003. The plague generation today. *The Science Teacher* 70 (7): 42–45.

10

Live Long and Prosper

And Remember You Are Responsible

> With each passing year, the public expects more of schools and teachers. Curriculums become more complex, student populations become more diverse, responsibilities are added, and, except for resources, very little is taken away. Fundamentally, teachers are held responsible for everyone and everything that goes on in their classrooms, an awesome responsibility—and a world of opportunity.

Four Ps for Professionals

You are the science teaching professional. You know your responsibilities include more than the education of your students. Even though you may see them only one period a day, you act in loco parentis—in a legal sense, in place of parents for the students assigned to you during the time they are scheduled to study with you. You can assume these responsibilities because you

▶ **Prepare:** Your formal education and studies are just the beginning of your professional training and development. You constantly keep up to date with continuing education by participating in professional organizations and by reading journals and research reports in education, instructional strategies, and subject areas. You make yourself thoroughly familiar with the learning expectations and standards set by federal, state, and local authorities, and take the time to analyze and compare them to other sources of information—recommendations of professional organizations, research data, and your own knowledge and training. You make sure you read and understand all school policies and procedures that relate to your duties and responsibilities, reviewing and filing new information and bulletins that update manuals and other official documents.

11

- ▶ Plan: You take the time to consider what you are required to teach and the best strategies to ensure your students can learn effectively and safely. You consult with support personnel so that you know the special needs of your students. You write out your plans, not just so others can read them, but so you can review and critique them yourself before you begin the lesson and remember what you've done later. If you have interns, student teachers, aides, parent volunteers, or guest speakers, you determine how best to prepare them to work safely with you and your students. You think ahead about the learning styles, maturity, and behavior of each of your students and determine the best way to work with their strengths and their limitations.

- ▶ Prevent: You take the time to assess hazards and review procedures for accident prevention. You read journals and check the material safety data sheets (MSDS) on the chemicals you buy. You teach and review safety procedures with every student and adult for hazards that might be anticipated. You post safety signs and keep copies of safety information. If you detect safety hazards you cannot ameliorate, you put your concerns and requests for assistance or changes in writing to the appropriate supervisor and modify your plans until the situations are remedied.

- ▶ Protect: You check your facilities for the presence and accessibility of correctly operating safety equipment and protective devices. You count the protective devices you have, such as safety glasses or aprons, to ensure you have enough in good condition for everyone who needs them. You demonstrate and instruct students and helpers on the proper use of safety equipment and protective gear. You keep records of safety lessons and instructions to ensure no one has missed getting the information. You insist on the use of protective devices by everyone in the room, including yourself and all visitors.

Broadening Your Definition of Safety

As classroom teacher and science teacher, you need to consider safety as broadly as possible. The prior chapters of this book are not intended to be an exhaustive manual of everything you must do or know to ensure safe science investigations. Rather, they are meant to sharpen your observational skills so you recognize the issues and circumstances that require your attention and planning in order for you to conduct science inquiry safely. No single book or series of books can anticipate all the safety issues that can arise in an active science program. Nor can any book, this one included, anticipate what new information and technology will render the advice given inaccurate or incorrect. It is the habit of observing and thinking about science lessons with common sense and safety in mind that will keep you and your students safe.

11

A Diversity of Needs

The population of students in high school science classes has become increasingly diverse. Not long ago, high school science classes above freshman level contained mostly students with the highest interest and ability in science. Today we find it critically important to offer all students a full range of investigative science experiences that lead to inquisitive habits of mind and safe practices in everyday life. A twenty-first century high school graduate—even one who does not intend to pursue a career in the sciences—will be faced, almost daily, with questions and decisions best made when informed by the ability to observe, gather, and analyze data, draw conclusions based on empirical evidence, and critically challenge previously accepted theories. Science every year for everybody in every high school might well be considered a safety requirement for a democratic society.

With less institutionalizing and modern medical technology, many students attending school have significant physical and psychological disabilities. Accommodation and modification for these students—all your students—are your legal and professional responsibility. You cannot delegate the responsibility to the special education department, nor can the special education department leave you to make adjustments all on your own. How do you prepare for special physical needs, special educational needs, and special behavioral needs? Under Public Law 94-142, also known as the Individuals with Disabilities Education Act (IDEA), it is your responsibility to read individual education plans (IEPs) and to meet the requirements defined in them. Your special education personnel are obligated to help explain IEP goals and objectives to you and help you design and implement appropriate accommodations when you request assistance.

Some students may have needs identified under Section 504 of the Americans with Disabilities Act (ADA). Even though they are not special education students, they are entitled to modifications; these are a general education legal responsibility. Chapter 2, "Communities of Learners," is devoted entirely to information to assist you in working with today's diverse community of learners.

Substitute Teachers, Interns, and Student Teachers

The actions of substitute teachers, interns, and student teachers in your classroom are also part of your responsibility. They are considered to be implementing your plans, your rules, and your instructions. Unless you are certain these people are able and qualified to conduct an activity safely and properly, do not plan active investigation for times you are not present. Keep a separate set of lesson plans that can be substituted for science lab activities if you should be absent unexpectedly. Do not ask your intern to be your substitute unless this practice is specifically authorized by your school.

11

Guests and Others

You also need to safeguard yourself and your students from well-meaning—or not-so-well-meaning—guests or intruders. In some schools, surprise guests and observers are commonplace. If this is the case, be sure all such people are first cleared by the school administration. All visitors should be required to check in with the school office as their first stop when arriving. This provides the school with a list of who is entering the building and gives visitors an opportunity to receive assistance in finding the person or location they need. On signing in, visitors should be issued a dated visitor name tag before proceeding onto the campus. The visitor must wear the tag so that anyone can see it. Check all visitors—familiar and unfamiliar—not only for the name tag, but also for the correct date on the tag. If either is missing, ask that the visitor return to the office or notify the office of the possible presence of an intruder. This procedure is particularly important if your class includes a student involved in a dispute about custody or guardianship.

For some schools, asking all guests to sign in may be a new concept. The school has always been a welcoming environment with an open door policy. No one wants to change or lose that warm spirit or let changing times send us into a bunker mentality, but asking all visitors to sign in does not have to change the ambience of the school. In the last analysis, registering your presence is just a courteous thing to do. And the person noting the registration can take the opportunity to extend a warm welcome. If a regular routine of meeting and greeting is established, it makes everyone feel welcome and ensures everyone is treated equally.

Sometimes school personnel may hesitate to ask or remind a parent or frequent visitor to sign in at the office and to bring a written okay from the office if a student is to be dismissed early. Actually, the chance that an untoward event will result from a stranger's actions is still very, very small. Statistically, the problematic situation is much more likely to result from the actions of someone well known to everyone and familiar with the school. In one real-life situation, a student's mother came to the classroom door and asked to speak to her son. Since the science teacher knew her well, he readily agreed. The student didn't come back. Unbeknownst to the teacher, there was a custody dispute going on. The mother kidnapped her son and took him to another state. Don't be shy about the rules—applying them to those known to you as well as to strangers is both fair and prudent.

> ### Dated Visitor Name Tags
>
> A variety of dated stickers is available to affix on temporary name tags. On some, a prominent pattern or logo develops on the name tag after 24 hours, making an expired tag very obvious.

Investigative science activities usually generate more excitement and more physical movement than most other activities, so it's best to avoid adding adult or student guests to these activities. Since you are

11

responsible for the safety of everyone present during laboratory investigations, you have the right to insist everyone acknowledge and comply with all safety procedures prior to joining or observing your class.

CLASSROOM GUESTS

In light of tragedies which have beset secondary schools in recent years, every staff member must be conscious of security every day. You are responsible for the conduct of everyone who enters your classroom—students as well as assistants and visitors. You have the right and responsibility to control who enters and to insist that your safety rules apply to everyone in your classroom. Those who have not been properly instructed on safe conduct must be excluded until the omission can be corrected.

Be sure you are aware of everyone who enters, who they are, and whether they have a legitimate reason for being in your room.

If you have a classroom door that opens directly to the outside, make sure that it can only be opened from the inside and students understand it may be opened only by or with the permission of a supervising adult inside the room.

During science lab activities that involve special techniques or safety precautions, admit only those who have been adequately instructed in and who are prepared to follow safe procedures. This includes supervisors, observers, and guests. They should come for the entire sequence of instruction or return at another time.

Students in your room should not be communicating with outside friends and others during school time. Students' cell phones and pagers, if they are permitted in the building, should be turned off and stored in the manner specified by your school's student manual.

- Schools are required to perform criminal offender record information (CORI) checks for every volunteer in the school. Those who have been approved should have a unique identification, indicating their purpose in the school. If you are planning to have a guest speaker, you need to explain the process and gain permission for the school to complete required security checks well ahead of the presentation date.

- If you are planning to have guest speakers, make sure you have thoroughly planned for their presentations and all safety issues have been addressed.

11

> ▶ Make sure that you have control or at least thorough knowledge of every-
> thing that occurs in your room when you are not there. If you must share a
> room, arrange for daily communication. If a night school program uses your
> room, establish ground rules and a regular system of communication.

Legal Responsibilities

In today's litigious society, you cannot prevent a lawsuit from being filed. No matter
how unreasonable the complaint, our legal system provides the opportunity for people
to take their grievances to court. Well-insured schools may be viewed as sources of
"deep pockets" and targets of frivolous suits. There are, however, many things you
can do to prevent being found at fault or liable.

The Jargon

If an accident occurs, a teacher can be engulfed in a maze of legal terms and procedures. You'll want legal support immediately. Understanding the basics of civil law
can help you avoid its pitfalls. Here are some simplified definitions:

▶ *Misfeasance*: Performance of a lawful action in an illegal or improper manner. In a
science activity, this might result from unintentionally using an incorrect chemical
for an experiment or too much of the correct chemical. It might include selecting
an activity inappropriate for the students to whom it was assigned or providing
incorrect instructions. The further you deviate from the recommended district
curriculum, the greater the risk you take on for yourself.

▶ *Negligence*: Failure to exercise appropriate care. (This could be called nonfeasance.)
This could include failure to warn students of safety hazards, to provide eye protection or fire equipment, or to practice a standard fire drill exit procedure. If you
had eye protection available, but did not make sure your students were using the
protection when needed, this could also be considered an omission and result in
liability. Being out of your room when your students are in class can create a nonfeasance liability. If students you are responsible for are working in an alcove, a
hall, or some part of the room where you cannot see and supervise them, you
could be accused of negligence.

▶ *Malfeasance*: Intentional wrongdoing, deliberate violation of law or standard, or
mismanagement of responsibilities. Ignorance is no excuse. If there is a governing
law or regulation, or local written policy, you are responsible for knowing about it
and conforming. Many states have benchmarks or standards that include safety
precautions and lessons. These can have the effect of law even though there is no
penalty statute. For example, an adopted state standard may require that you teach
some safety procedure but neglect to specify a penalty if you do not. In the event
of an accident that might have been prevented with the safety procedure, your

11

failure to teach the procedure may not result in a criminal charge against you, but it could be construed as malfeasance for which you could be found liable.

▶ *Tort:* A wrong you do to someone. If you give students the wrong instructions or fail to provide appropriate safe instructions for performing an activity and the activity results in accident or injury, your action is a tort.

▶ *Liability:* The potential responsibility for damage; the civil obligation not to commit a wrong.

CASES THAT INFORM

The following are composite "cases" based on lawsuits that have actually occurred. Although each situation is different and we have omitted many details, these scenarios highlight issues you may confront.

A high school student was severely burned when an alcohol burner which she was using ignited her shirt. The teacher was present, and had warned students to be careful with the burners. Was the teacher held liable? Yes, because alcohol burners are illegal in many states and strongly discouraged in the safety literature for our profession. The teacher should have known that alcohol burners were now considered unsafe, even though they had been purchased years earlier by her school.

A school scheduled a science class in a mathematics classroom. The teacher informed the principal in writing that the room was unsuitable for investigative science activities and then proceeded to conduct the district hands-on science program. An accident occurred during a lab activity in the room. Who was liable? Both the school and the teacher, because the teacher could not abrogate her duty to protect students by simply writing a memo. Even though you notify your administrator of a problem, you are not off the hook. You must demonstrate that you've changed your program to avoid the risk.

On a field trip, a teacher identified a snake as nonvenomous, and students brought it back to the classroom, where it was housed in the preparation room in a terrarium labeled "Danger—Snake." A few days later some students were working in the preparation room unsupervised, and the snake bit one of them. The student required emergency treatment for the snakebite. Was the teacher liable? Yes, because the students in the preparation room were not directly and appropriately supervised.

11

The Best Defense

Sounds intimidating? Perhaps, but you can reduce your exposure to these liabilities dramatically by adopting some relatively straightforward policies. Here are some tips:

▶ Document your preparation for safety. Subscribe to journals, read books, and take classes to keep up-to-date. Online courses on safety may be convenient and timely.

▶ As part of your lesson plans and records, document safety instruction. Make sure you keep records of follow-up with safety lessons for students who are absent. Repeat the lessons individually with students who transfer into the class. Keep records of rules given to students and records of disciplinary action with rules violators.

▶ Do not leave the premises when you are responsible for students. Never—not even if you have a student teacher. Do not permit students to work where they are out of your sight and supervision or send them on errands. This can result in a serious liability.

▶ Put your safety needs in writing. Don't just complain: Explain why equipment and maintenance needs are necessary. (Buy your administrator a copy of this book, if necessary.) Associate each request with the hands-on experiences that would be possible if it were fulfilled. Follow up on your requests. Don't stop until the situation is corrected.

▶ Do not engage in any activity involving a reported safety hazard until the hazard is mitigated. Modify your labs until the corrections have been made and keep a record of the changes you are making. That doesn't mean do nothing. Use smaller quantities. Break labs into subunits. Ask for a coteacher so you can work with half the class at one time. Each of these modifications indicates you are acting as a reasonable and prudent professional.

▶ If you are facing possible litigation, collect your records and your recollections immediately. Make sure you have the advice, and possibly the presence, of an attorney who represents your interests before making any statements to anyone else. Consult your teachers' association as well as the administration.

Documents to Keep Up-to-Date

▶ District policy manuals and all subsequent policy communications
▶ State and local curriculum guides
▶ Lesson plan book
▶ Attendance and grade book—with correlations to the lesson plan book and records of safety lessons for each individual student
▶ Inventory of materials and equipment
▶ Maintenance requests
▶ Purchase requisitions with MSDSs
▶ Records and notes of professional development activities

11

Insurance

Lawsuits are expensive even if they are dismissed or you are found not to be responsible. It can take months and cost tens of thousands of dollars just to get a nuisance suit in front of a judge so you can have it dismissed. There will be accusations, investigations, and depositions. That's why insurance is vital.

Begin by investigating what coverage you already have. Most school systems have errors and omissions coverage for the institution and its employees. This will cover mistakes. Some states require districts to indemnify and hold harmless their teachers, but policies and regulations may have exemptions and exclusions. Find out what the exceptions are. Insurance policies generally exclude any action that violates the law, and that can be the catch-22. If the law says you must teach the fire drill procedure or prohibits the use of alcohol burners, you may find yourself without insurance coverage if you violate the law. Most district policies cover employees, but they may not cover consultants, volunteers, or visitors. You would not be covered for a job, such as working as a scout leader or curriculum consultant, in which you were moonlighting.

You may have liability insurance through your union or professional association. In general, these policies will cover the preliminary costs of a lawsuit. They will get you a lawyer quickly, separate from the one that represents the district, and get you preliminary advice. But many of these policies exclude any punitive damages, so the cost of your lawyer may be covered but not the biggest part of a future settlement.

Many teachers carry extra professional coverage through their professional association, homeowner's, or renter's policy. You may be able to obtain an umbrella policy to extend coverage and back up other liability policies you may have. Your coverage might be a rider for professional liability on an existing policy, usually at very little additional cost. Extra coverage is highly recommended.

Take Heart

With all this talk of litigation and liability you may be asking, "Is inquiry worth it?" The answer is, "Yes, absolutely." A teacher who maintains his or her professional development, plans carefully, embeds safety training all year long, and properly supervises every student has little to fear. When you take time to prepare for safely conducting an active investigative science program, you not only assist your students in answering the questions on their next test, but you also prepare your students to answer future questions we have yet to imagine. Your habit of conducting work thoughtfully and safely becomes the model for the conduct of your students at home and in their future endeavors. As the first teacher in space, Christa McAuliffe, so elegantly put it, we touch the future when we teach.

11

THE SAVVY SCIENCE TEACHER

Mr. H was rarely afraid. He climbed rock walls, canoed white water, and rode roller coasters. But the day he realized that part of his chemical inventory was missing, a frisson of fear ran through him.

He first suspected something was wrong when he prepped for a lab. A dustless circle in the corrosives cabinet told him to check his inventory. A few keystrokes and his Inventory program told him what had happened: A liter of concentrated HCl had disappeared.

Mr. H immediately notified the principal and the custodian. He pulled the MSDS on the missing chemical from the computer and verified that the stock was fresh and concentrated—very dangerous in the wrong hands. Together they checked the locks. There was no sign of forced entry. But the HCl was most assuredly gone.

A police detective was called in to investigate. "Who might have had keys to this storeroom?" she asked. "Only science teachers," both Mr. H and his boss answered simultaneously. Almost immediately, they also realized that former science teachers might still have keys. They made a quick list. Dr. J had retired, and turned in his keys right before leaving. But how about Ms. K? She had once taught freshman physical science, but was now teaching in her major, art.

A flash of insight prompted the principal to make a phone call. Yes, Ms. K had entered the storeroom and taken the acid to etch jewelry for a master's project. The incident prompted a disciplinary hearing and a change in procedure. From now on, all keys would be returned and accounted for at the end of each school year. Thanks to good records and alert monitoring, a mystery was solved without risk to staff or students.

11

Connections

▶ This book has become the basis for an online course in safety that is a good review for all teachers and their supervisors. Check the National Science Teachers Association website at *www.nsta.org* for more information.

▶ Law Dictionary. See *dictionary.law.com.*

▶ Legal Principles. See *www.ric.edu/ptiskus/ liability.htm.*

▶ Sample of Chemical Classroom Accidents. See *www.safechem.com/ Campusafe/accident.htm.*

▶ Overcrowding in the laboratory. See *www.flinn sci.com/homepage/ safe/ovrcrowd.html.*

11

Conclusion

Review the Basics

Teaching is a multifaceted, complex process. You make dozens of instructional decisions each hour. You manage an environment, a curriculum, and a community of learners. Safety issues must be an integral part of science instruction and embedded in every laboratory and field activity. This book has taken a broad view of factors that should be considered when preparing for a safe investigative science program. To relate these ideas to reality, we have included anecdotes—some almost verbatim and some composites—of actual experiences of teachers and supervisors. They are meant to illustrate both the risks and the opportunities in the familiar environment of your science room.

We hope these ideas have sharpened your perceptions, raised your safety antennae, and also demonstrated that the best safety advice is heightening your awareness rather than merely following rules that may become outdated. Here are some general principles that may be drawn from each of the chapters:

1 Setting the Scene

- ▶ Rather than confining safety issues to an introductory unit, introduce safe procedures with each exploration and repeat relevant safety instructions with each subsequent activity.

- ▶ Model the safe behaviors you expect your students to practice.

- ▶ Have students share responsibility for monitoring safe procedures so that safe work habits become second nature.

- ▶ Make administrators and facilities staff part of your safety team. Educate them about the conditions and facilities needed to teach science safely.

- ▶ Modify your curriculum to conform to the conditions of your facilities and the nature of your students and classes.

2 Communities of Learners

- ▶ In planning laboratory activities, provide modifications and accommodations to ensure they are maximally accessible to all students.

- ▶ Eliminate barriers in your room, including removing clutter and freeing up space.

- Read and incorporate individual education plan (IEP) recommendations for students who have IEPs.

- Communicate with administrators and special needs staff to obtain support and suggestions for modifying your program for special needs students.

- Minimize the potential for disruptive behavior with shorter and more specific tasks.

- Request appropriate support staff and aides for students who need them. Plan time to train these assistants.

- Investigate the use of adaptive equipment and technologies with consultants and district support staff.

3 Where Science Happens

- Conduct science activities in facilities that provide adequate space and ventilation for safety.

- Check for appropriate utilities and safety equipment for all laboratory activities. If items or conditions are not adequate, modify your curriculum to ensure that the only activities you conduct are activities that can be done safely.

- Select furniture that is stable but easily rearranged, and provide unobstructed flat work surfaces.

- Ensure that safety equipment such as fire extinguishers, fire blankets, safety showers, and eyewashes are operational and accessible.

- Check that electrical service and wiring to your room are well maintained, provide adequate amperage, and include appropriate ground-fault interrupter (GFI) protection.

4 Finders Keepers

- Use well-organized and clearly marked open shelves to store supplies and equipment that students are to obtain and return on their own. Arrange the material so that a missing item is easily spotted without counting individual items.

- Include enough locked storage, inaccessible to students, for valuable and fragile supplies and equipment as well as materials too hazardous for direct student access.

- Store all chemical stocks in locked cabinets and locked chemical storerooms appropriately equipped and off limits to students.

- Keep incompatible chemicals separated—arrange storage by chemical properties, not by alphabetical order.

- Maintain accurate, up-to-date, and regularly reviewed chemical inventories.

- Maintain materials safety data sheets (MSDS) for every product—one set in the office and one set at the storage-and-use location.

- Prepare materials and supplies for science activities in an adequate, ventilated, and well-lit preparation space away from student and other traffic.

- Clear out excess supplies, equipment, and furniture regularly as a vital part of safe practice.

5 Lively Science

- Maintain living cultures to provide students with opportunities for activities involving observation and care of living organisms and biological systems.

- Choose organisms appropriate for the space and time available. Ensure that adequate safety and security are available and that you can maintain the organism in a healthy environment over weekends and extended vacation periods.

- Begin with simple organisms—plants and invertebrates—before trying to maintain more complex and difficult ones.

- Do not bring wild or feral animals, dead or alive, into the classroom.

- Avoid organisms that are toxic, highly allergenic, or temperamental.

- Inform students, parents, and colleagues who share facilities of your cultures and be aware of unusual allergies.

- In shared spaces, ensure that all users agree to provide appropriate safety and security before introducing a living organism.

- Do not release, introduce, or plant non-native species in the open environment. Avoid the use of exotic species if at all possible.

6 Modern Alchemy

- Emphasize careful scientific process skills over drama.

- Use microscale experiments for safety and to encourage careful observation.

- Choose less toxic and less hazardous options over traditional labs now known to be dangerous.

- Maintain a minimal quantity and variety of chemicals—less is better.

- Require the use of appropriate safety equipment by all persons—students and adults—at all times.

- Consider the problems and costs of disposal before purchasing any chemical reagent.
- Use professional hazardous waste removal services as appropriate.

7 Striking Gold

- Before beginning activities, instruct students on safe procedures and safety mechanisms for tools and equipment.
- Never allow the tasting of specimens.
- Avoid contact with and use of contaminated soils, and insist on proper hand washing.
- Never permit direct observation of the Sun.
- Review rules and safety procedures prior to field studies.

8 Falling for Science

- Before beginning activities, instruct students on safe procedures and safety mechanisms for tools and equipment.
- Use light and sound experiments as an opportunity to discuss preventing damage to eyes and ears.
- Make sure all electrical connections are safe and conform to code.
- Plan ahead so your room won't have physical barriers such as loose cords and other tripping and falling hazards.

9 The Great Outdoors

- Link field trips and field studies to curriculum goals.
- Preview the site and abutting properties before planning your field study.
- Determine proper clothing and footwear for the site and activities planned.
- Meet with cooperating resource people to plan activities.
- Orient and train all chaperones in your planned activities and in safety precautions.
- Plan appropriate accommodations for special needs and physically disabled students.

10 The Kitchen Sink

▶ Minimize the use of carpets and upholstered furniture to reduce the growth and harboring of dust mites, mold spores, and other allergens.

▶ Regularly and carefully clean living cultures in the room.

▶ Check for the presence of heavy-metal contamination from prior activities—remove and appropriately dispose of all mercury and mercury-based instruments.

▶ Review appropriate clothing, covering, and protective eyewear for laboratory work.

▶ Ensure supervision in using the Internet.

▶ Obtain consent forms before photographing students.

▶ Never prepare food or eat in science lab areas.

▶ Participate in first aid training and crisis response training.

▶ Communicate with parents.

▶ Plan with others for appropriate class sizes and scheduling, and adequate space and materials for an investigative science program.

▶ Make safety and security a significant concern of all staff.

11 Live Long and Prosper

▶ Prepare, plan, prevent, and protect.

▶ Become familiar with school policies and federal, state, and local laws.

▶ Document all safety-related activities including instructions provided to each student and assistant.

▶ Assess your safety lessons, and keep detailed records.

▶ Take responsibility to supervise and train your assistants and volunteers.

▶ Make sure you are adequately protected with liability insurance.

References

Adler, D. A., N. Tobin (Illustrator). 1999. *How tall, how short, how faraway*. New York, NY: Holiday House.

American Association for the Advancement of Science. 1991. *Barrier free in brief: Laboratories and classrooms in science and engineering*. Washington, DC: AAAS.

American Chemical Society and ACS Board—Council Committee on Chemical Safety. 2001. *Chemical safety for teachers and their supervisors*. Washington, DC: ACS. Available in PDF format at *membership.acs.org/c/ccs/pubs/chemical_safety_manual.pdf*

Biehle, J., L. Motz, and S. West. 1999. *NSTA guide to science facilities*. Arlington, VA: NSTA Press.

Colburn, Alan. 2003. *The lingo of learning: 88 education terms every science teacher should know*. Arlington, VA: NSTA Press.

Flinn Scientific Catalog/Reference Manual. 2002. Batavia, IL: Flinn Scientific, Inc. See *www.flinnsci.com*

Foster, G. W. 1999. *Elementary mathematics and science methods: Inquiry teaching and learning*. Belmont, CA: Wadsworth Publishing Co.

Hallowell, E. M., and J. J. Ratey. 1995. *Driven to distraction.* New York: Pantheon Books.

Keteyian, L. 2001. A garden story. *Science and Children* 39 (3): 22–25.

Levine, M., 2002. *A mind at a time.* New York: Simon and Schuster.

Lowery, L., ed. 2000. Appendix C in *NSTA pathways to the science standards—elementary school edition*. Arlington, VA: NSTA Press.

McCullough, J., and R. McCullough. 2000. *The role of toys in teaching physics*. College Park, MD: American Association of Physics Teachers.

Merck and Co., Inc. 2001. *The Merck Index.* Published annually. Rahway, NJ: The Merck Publishing Group. See *www.merck.com* for CD-ROM and online versions.

National Research Council. 1996. *National science education standards*. Washington, DC: National Academy Press. Online version at *www.nap.edu/books/0309053269/html/index.html*

Reese, K. M. 1985. *Teaching chemistry to physically handicapped students*. Washington, DC: American Chemical Society.

Robertson, W. C. 2001. *Community connections for science education: Building successful partnerships*. Arlington, VA: NSTA Press.

Roy, K., P. Markow, and J. Kaufman. 2001. *Safety is elementary: The new standard for safety in the elementary science classroom.* Natick, MA: The Laboratory Safety Institute.

Russell, H. R. 2001. *Ten-minute field trips.* Arlington, VA: NSTA Press.

Sarquis, M. 2000. *Building student safety habits for the workplace.* Middletown, OH: Terrific Science Press.

Sprenger, M. B. 2002. *Becoming a "wiz" at brain-based teaching: How to make every year your best year.* Thousand Oaks, CA: Corwin Press, Inc.

Wood, C. G. 1995. *Safety in school science labs.* Natick, MA: Kaufman and Associates.

Web Resources

As teachers of science we promote a healthy dose of skepticism. We encourage our students not just to seek information but also to think for themselves and question what is presented. We encourage you the reader to use that same caution in using the list of websites we have presented. To our knowledge they are as they profess to be; however, we urge you to make your own decisions as to their validity and usefulness. Websites change with time. We offer these sites not as a bona fide list, one of certainty, but as a list of starting points—possible sources of information.

The websites that are accessed through NSTA's SciLinks program are continually reviewed and updated.

Chapter 1: Setting the Scene

National Research Council. 1996. *National science education standards*. Washington, DC: National Academy Press. Online version at *www.nap.edu/books/0309053269/ html/index.html*

Laboratory Safety Institute. James A. Kaufman, President. *www.labsafety.org/about.htm*

AAAS, American Association for the Advancement of Science *www.aaas.org*

NABT, National Association of Biology Teachers *www.nabt.org*

MSDS for Infectious Substances, Health Canada *www.hc-sc.gc.ca/pphb-dgspsp/msds-ftss/index.html*

Chapter 2: Communities of Learners

IDEA, Individuals with Disabilities Education Act *www.ed.gov/offices/OSERS/Policy/IDEA/index.html* *www4.law.cornell.edu/uscode/20/1400.html*

ADA, The Americans with Disabilities Act *www.usdoj.gov/crt/ada/adahom1.htm* *(www.usdoj.gov/crt/ada/pubs/ada.txt)*

SC*i*LINKS.
THE WORLD'S A CLICK AWAY
Topic: learners with disabilities
Go to: *www.scilinks.org*
Code: SHL16

CEC, The Council for Exceptional Children
www.cec.sped.org

West Virginia University
Inclusion in Science Education for Students with Disabilities
www.as.wvu.edu/~scidis

Chapter 3: Where Science Happens

EPA, Environmental Protection Agency IAQ INFO, 800-438-4318.
www.epa.gov

SIRI, Vermont Safety Information Resources, Inc.
www.siri.org/

MSDS (Materials Safety Data Sheet)
www.flinnsci.com/homepage/cindex.html
esf.uvm.edu/uvmsafety/labsafety/chemsafety/netmsds.html
msds.pdc.cornell.edu/msdssrch.asp

NFPA, National Fire Protection Association
www.nfpa.org/catalog/home/index.asp

NFPA 101, Life Safety Code
www.nfpa.org/BuildingCode/AboutC3/NFPA101/nfpa101.asp

NFPA 45, Standard on Fire Protection for Laboratories Using Chemicals
www.nfpa.org/Codes/NFPA_Codes_and_Standards/List_of_NFPA_documents/
NFPA_45.asp

NFPA 5000, Building Construction and Safety Code
www.nfpa.org/catalog/product.asp?pid=500003&target%5Fpid=500003&
link%5Ftype=search&src=nfpa

ANSI Z87.1, American National Standards Institute
www.ansi.org
www1.ivenue.com/coltslaboratories/filecabinet/ansicompar.pdf

OSHA, Occupational Safety and Health Administration
www.osha.gov
www.osha.gov/comp-links.html

OSHA, Hazard Communication
www.osha.gov/SLTC/hazardcommunications/index.html

OSHA Regulations (Standards - 29 CFR) "Laboratory Standards" Occupational
Exposure to Hazardous Chemicals in Laboratories - 1910.1450
*www.osha.gov/pls/oshaweb/owadisp.show_document?p_table=STANDARDS&
p_id=10106*

OSHA Regulations (Standards - 29 CFR) "Chemical Hygiene Officer and Program"
National Research Council Recommendations Concerning Chemical Hygiene in
Laboratories (Non-Mandatory) - 1910.1450 App. A
*www.osha.gov/pls/oshaweb/owadisp.show_document?p_table=STANDARDS&
p_id=10107*

NIOSH, National Institute for Occupational Safety and Health
Chemical Safety
www.cdc.gov/niosh/topics/chemical-safety

Fume Hoods Fact Sheet, Office of Environmental Health and Safety, University of
California Berkeley, 11 September 2003
www.ehs.berkeley.edu/pubs/factsheets/09fumehd.html

American Society for Microbiology
Hand Washing Information
www.microbe.org/washup/Wash_Up.asp

Chapter 4: Finders Keepers

Cornell University Environmental Health
www.ehs.cornell.edu

The EPA is responsible for hazardous waste
www.epa.gov/ebtpages/wastes.html

Vermont Safety Information Resources, Inc.
See *siri.uvm.edu/msds*.

Chapter 5: Lively Science

American Society for Microbiology
www.microbe.org

SC*i*INKS.
THE WORLD'S A CLICK AWAY

Topic: chemical safety
Go to: *www.scilinks.org*
Code: SHL51

SC*i*INKS.
THE WORLD'S A CLICK AWAY

Topic: bacteria
Go to: *www.scilinks.org*
Code: SHL70

Topic: protista
Go to: *www.scilinks.org*
Code: SHL71A

Topic: invertebrates
Go to: *www.scilinks.org*
Code: SHL72

Topic: fungi
Go to: *www.scilinks.org*
Code: SHL71B

Topic: viruses
Go to: *www.scilinks.org*
Code: SHL74

PTC Tasting
physchem.ox.ac.uk/MSDS/PH/1-phenyl-2-thiourea.html

Chapter 6: Modern Alchemy

National Microscale Chemisty Center
www.microscale.org/about.asp

American Chemical Society and ACS Board-Council Committee on Chemical
Safety. 2001. *Chemical Safety for Teachers and Their Supervisors*.
Washington, DC
membership.acs.org/c/ccs/pubs/chemical_safety_manual.pdf

Chapter 7: Striking Gold

Topic: astronomy
Go to: *www.scilinks.org*
Code: SHL102

Chapter 8: Falling for Science

The International Electrical Safety Foundation
www.esfi.org/index.php

Topic: electricity
Go to: *www.scilinks.org*
Code: SHL109

Chapter 9: The Great Outdoors

Centers for Disease Control
www.cdc.gov
www.cdc.gov/travel
www.cdc.gov/travel/yb/index.htm

Department of State
travel.state.gov/travel_warnings.html

Annenberg Amusement Park Physics 2003.
www.learner.org/exhibits/parkphysics/

Robertson, W. C. 2001. *Community Connections for Science Education: Building Successful Partnerships.* Arlington, VA: NSTA Press.
www.nsta.org/main/pdfs/store/PB160X1np.pdf

Chapter 10: The Kitchen Sink

NCLBA, The No Child Left Behind Act
www.ed.gov/nclb/landing.jhtml

NIOSH, National Institute for Occupational Safety and Health
www.cdc.gov/niosh

Chapter 11: Live Long and Prosper

Law Dictionary
dictionary.law.com/

Overcrowding in the Laboratory
www.flinnsci.com/homepage/safe/ovrcrowd.html

Glossary

Discussion of the topic is indicated in parentheses. Use the index to find specific text using the terms.

ADA: The Americans with Disabilities Act of 1990. This act requires that physical and other accommodations be made to enable all individuals to have access to physical facilities, education, and employment. (Chapter 2, p. 19)

ANSI Z87.1: American National Standards Institute recommended standard for impact-resistant safety eyewear. The Occupational Safety and Health Administration (OSHA) has made the standard a requirement. (Chapter 10, p. 147)

bloodborne disease: Human illnesses that can be transmitted via contact with infected human blood. These include Hepatitis B, Hepatitis C, and HIV-AIDS. (Chapter 10, p. 142)

carcinogen: A substance that can cause cancer. Many laboratory chemicals, such as formaldehyde, can be carcinogenic and should be avoided or used very carefully at the high school level. Material safety data sheets (MSDS) and the Merck Index can be used to check for carcinogenic properties of chemicals.

combustible: A substance that ignites and burns easily, such as paper or cardboard.

conjunctivitis: Highly infectious inflammation of the conjunctiva of the eye that can be caused either by bacteria or viruses. Commonly referred to as "pink eye," it can be easily transmitted between users of safety eyewear or optical eyepieces. (Chapter 10, p. 147)

CDC: Centers for Disease Control and Prevention. A federal agency responsible for tracking, investigating, and recommending methods to contain the incidence of diseases in the population, including diseases that may be acquired outside the United States. (Chapter 9, p. 133)

CORI check: Criminal offender record information check. Many states or municipalities have regulations that require schools to perform a check of CORI databases before persons may be permitted to interact with students. This can include potential employees and adult volunteers and guests.

cyanoacrylic glue: A class of glues known by a variety of trade names such as SuperGlue or Krazy Glue.

DEET: Diethyl toluamide. The active ingredient in many insect repellents. Some people may be allergic to the compound. (Chapter 9, p. 126)

Discrepant event: An unanticipated or unexpected result. Major scientific breakthroughs are often the result of scientists noticing a discrepant event that otherwise

187

might be considered an accident or "failed" experiment. A classic example is Fleming's discovery of the anitibiotic effects of penicillin when the mold accidentally contaminated his culture dish.

endangered species: Organisms that are protected by federal, state, or local regulations because their populations are so low that survival of the species is in jeopardy. Protections include prohibitions on collection, killing, or disruption of breeding grounds or territories.

EPA: Environmental Protection Agency. There are both federal and state EPAs that promulgate and enforce regulations to protect the environment.

exotic species: Species that are not native to or naturally found in the environment they are in. These include imported plants and animals as well as plants and animals that may be from closer locations but introduced to environments that lack natural competitors or predators. (Chapter 5, p. 74)

filtering software: Computer programs that are installed to block access to Internet websites that may be considered to have unacceptable content such as pornography, hate literature, or terrorist information. These programs usually operate by checking for words or phrases and are frequently ineffective or problematic because they do not block some sites that would be harmful or they block useful sites that legitimately use terms such as "vagina." We strongly recommend that you closely supervise students' Internet use and not rely on filtering software for protection. (Chapter 10, p. 149)

flammable: A substance that ignites easily and is capable of burning rapidly, such as alcohol or gasoline.

GFI protection: Ground-fault interrupter protection cuts the flow of electricity in cases of short circuit such as when an appliance is dropped into water. All electrical circuits in science areas should be protected. (Chapter 8, p. 110)

hazardous waste: Chemical and biological waste which requires special handling— usually governed by federal, state, or local regulation—for disposal. This includes agents that can cause harm to humans, animals, plants, or the environment. (Chapter 10, p. 140, 142–143)

hepatitis: Several infectious diseases of the liver, some of which are transmitted by human body fluids or food and water. In some cases, infectious carriers do not show active signs of the disease. Standard (Universal) Precautions and thorough hand washing should be used to prevent transmission. (Chapter 10, p. 141)

high-stakes tests: Tests for students—usually multiple-choice or short-answer types— that can result in serious consequences if not passed. These include tests mandated by individual states which high school students must pass in order to receive a high school diploma. Under the federal No Child Left Behind Act of 2001, the federal government required that students pass these state-mandated tests in order to receive federal grants and loans for higher education. Other examples of high-stakes tests include those that are administered to students, the results of which are used to rate school districts, schools for purposes of providing or withholding funds, and teachers for purposes of salary adjustments and dismissal. (Chapter 10, p. 158)

HIV: Human immunodeficiency virus, a retrovirus which is the causative agent of AIDS (acquired immunodeficiency syndrome).

human body fluids: Blood, saliva, vomitus, semen, and other fluids produced by the human body. Most are known to transmit disease and must be handled with Standard (Universal) Precautions. (Chapter 10, p. 142)

IDEA (PL 94-142): The Individuals with Disabilities Education Act, also known as Public Law 94-142. IDEA mandates that students with disabilities that prevent them from reaching their potential in education be provided with accessory materials and services. It also requires that, to the greatest extent possible, students with disabilities be educated with students who do not have disabilities. (Chapter 2, p. 17)

impact-resistant goggles: Safety eyewear that conforms to ANSI Z87.1 standards and provides impact protection. Impact-resistant goggles may or may not also provide chemical splash protection. We recommend that all safety eyewear provide both chemical splash and impact protection. (Chapter 10, p. 146)

inflammable: Same as flammable, but often mistaken to mean not capable of burning. To avoid confusion, we suggest not using the term "inflammable."

laboratory refrigerator: A refrigerator specifically designed not to emit sparks when cycling on so as to reduce explosion risks from volatile chemicals stored inside. It is significantly different from a household refrigerator. Any refrigerator—laboratory or household—used to store laboratory material should never be used to store food for human consumption.

laser: Light amplified by stimulated emission of radiation. Devices that emit this type of light must be used with extreme care to protect from exposure that can cause severe damage to eyes, skin, and other tissues. (Chapter 8, p. 109)

LD_{50}: Lethal Dose 50. The dose of a toxic substance that results in the death of 50% of test animals. (Chapter 6, p. 92)

material safety data sheet: MSDS. A standard document written in English and containing certain types of information available for every hazardous chemical manufactured or sold in the United States. It contains information that users and emergency personnel need to make appropriate decisions quickly. Federal and many state laws require that MSDSs be available all the time for every chemical you use or store. Administrative and noninstructional staff, teachers, students, and emergency responders must have easy access to them. (Chapter 4, p. 52)

mutagen: A substance or agent such as ultraviolet radiation that can increase the frequency of mutation in cells. The mutations may then result in cancer. Chemicals, such as some used in DNA studies, can be mutagenic and should not be used at the high school level. Material safety data sheets (MSDS) and the Merck Index can be used to check for mutagenic properties of chemicals.

National Science Education Standards: Goals for instruction, assessment, professional development, content, and programs in science education published in 1996 by the National Research Council, the administrative unit of the National Academy of Sciences. These standards were the result of a landmark effort by teachers, scientists, science educators, and other experts to define what science students should know and be able to do. They offer a coherent vision of what it means to be scientifically literate. (Chapter 2, p. 15)

NFPA: National Fire Protection Association. This international nonprofit group attempts to reduce fire and related hazards by gaining consensus and acceptance of codes and standards, research, training, and education.

NIOSH: National Institute for Occupational Safety and Health. Created by the Occupational Safety and Health Act of 1970, NIOSH is the federal agency established to research workplace safety and educate people about it. NIOSH is part of the Centers for Disease Control and Prevention in the Department of Health and Human Services.

No Child Left Behind Act of 2001: NCLBA. This omnibus federal legislation adopted in 2001 imposes requirements on institutions—public and some private—receiving federal education funds. The legislation includes requiring students to meet state-designed standards, usually in the form of high-stakes tests, to receive federal higher education grants and loans. It also requires districts to report the state certification and training status of all teachers they employ, and the number of classes that are taught by teachers not appropriately certified and "highly qualified" to teach the subject and to make this information available to the public. "Highly qualified" and certification are left to the individual states to define. By the end of the 2005–6 academic year, in order to receive federal funding, all teachers in the district must be certified and deemed "highly qualified" in any core academic course that they teach. The sciences are core academic courses. (Chapter 10, p. 158)

nonlatex: Made of a rubberlike material other than latex rubber, often nitrile. Latex rubber has been found to be dangerously allergenic to some individuals and can result in reactions severe enough to cause death. For this reason, we recommend that all "rubber" items such as rubber gloves, rubber tubing, and rubber stoppers be nonlatex. Nonlatex gloves should be available for cleanup of human body fluids using Standard (Universal) Precautions.

non-native species: Species that are not naturally found in the environment they are in. These include imported plants and animals as well as plants and animals that may be from closer locations but introduced to environments that lack natural competitors or predators. (Chapter 5, p. 74)

NRC: The National Research Council is the administrative unit of the National Academy of Sciences. It was the coordinating agency for the development of the National Science Education Standards. (Chapter 2, p. 15)

OSHA: Occupational Safety and Health Administration. Created by the Occupational Safety and Health Act of 1970, OSHA is the federal agency responsible for developing and enforcing workplace safety and health regulations.

potable water: Water that is fit for human consumption. Many buildings with older plumbing have excessive concentrations of lead in the water, rendering it hazardous to drink or use in food preparation.

prep room: A preparation room, situated close to the science room, preferably with direct access to the science room via a separately lockable door, in which a science teacher can prepare and securely store materials for science laboratory activities. For safety and security reasons, chemical stock supplies should never be stored in preparation rooms. Students should not be allowed in preparation areas without the direct supervision of their teacher. (Chapter 3, p. 29, and Chapter 4, p. 148)

safety eyewear: This phrase is used to represent a variety of ANSI Z87.1-compliant equipment for protection of the eyes including safety glasses, impact-resistant safety goggles, and chemical splash safety goggles. It does not include regular eyeglasses or plastic spectacles (also called "plant visitor specs"), which are not acceptable substitutes for either impact or chemical splash eye protection. (Chapter 10, p. 146)

safety goggles: Safety eyewear that complies with the ANSI Z87.1 standard and fits snugly to the face. These devices provide chemical splash protection AND/or impact protection. The term does not include regular eyeglasses, safety glasses, or plastic spectacles (also called "plant visitor specs"), which are not acceptable substitutes for either impact or chemical splash eye protection. (Chapter 10, p. 146)

science room: In this book, science room refers to any room in which science classes are instructed. In some cases, these are rooms outfitted for both lecture and laboratory work— the ideal. In other cases, a science room is for lecture or for laboratory work alone. A science room that is a general classroom used by science classes is a very risky practice. The term specifically excludes science storage rooms and science preparation rooms, because students should never be permitted in chemical storage rooms and, as a general rule, should not have access to science storage and preparation areas. (Chapter 3)

SPF: Sun protective factor. A measure of the potency of sunscreens and sunblocks in blocking ultraviolet (UV) radiation. Sunscreens with SPFs between 15 and 30 will block most UV radiation, according to the National Cancer Institute. (Chapter 9, p. 128)

splash goggles: Safety eyewear that prevents liquid splashes from entering the eyes. This eyewear fits snugly to the face and usually has baffles that allow air to circulate while protecting against liquid splash. If the baffles are removed or flipped open, the splash protection is compromised. Chemical splash goggles must conform to the ANSI Z87.1 standard and provide impact protection. We recommend that all safety eyewear provide both chemical splash and impact protection. (Chapter 10, p. 147)

Standard Precautions: Procedures that must be followed in order to prevent the transmission of diseases via contact with human body fluids. They incorporate Universal Precautions, and are referred to in this book as Standard (Universal) Precautions. (Chapter 10, p. 142)

storeroom: A storage room, situated close to the science room, preferably with direct access to the science room via a separately lockable door, in which supplies for the science program can be stored. All chemical stocks should be in storerooms dedicated to and equipped solely for the safe storage of chemicals. Students should never be allowed in chemical storerooms. (Chapter 3, p. 29, and Chapter 4, p. 48)

talc: A fine-grained mineral with a soapy feel. Crushed talc was once used to prepare talcum powder, face powder, and some types of short-grained rice. Since discovery that the mineral is often associated with carcinogenic asbestos fibers, it has largely been replaced by cornstarch.

teratogen: A substance that can cause malformations of an embryo or fetus. Many chemicals, including some frequently used biological stains, can be teratogenic and should not be used at the high school level. Material safety data sheets (MSDS) and the Merck Index can be used to check for teratogenic properties of chemicals.

Universal Precautions: Procedures that must be followed in order to prevent the transmission of human bloodborne diseases. This book refers to them as Standard (Universal) Precautions. The newer Standard Precautions incorporate Universal Precautions. (Chapter 10, p. 142)

UV: Ultraviolet radiation. A component of sunlight that can cause damage to the skin and retina. Excessive exposure to UV radiation may be responsible for an increased risk of skin cancer and cataracts years later. (Chapter 9, p. 128)

video cam: A video camera that can be mounted on a microscope or other optical instrument to send signals to a projection device that permits the whole class to observe an event that might otherwise be too small for everyone to observe simultaneously.

Appendix A

Chemicals to Go—Candidates for Disposal

The chemicals in the following table were once used in programs and demonstrations. They now are generally considered too hazardous to store and use in precollege programs. You should check the materials you have in your classroom and stockroom. Anything you do not need for your program should be removed. If your program requires any of the chemicals in this table, you should review the hazards involved and make sure you have the expertise, training, facilities, protective equipment, and sufficiently mature students to ensure the education benefits outweigh the risks. Consider replacing these chemicals with a safer alternative.

Most of these chemicals require special handling and special disposal. If you find these, or other hazardous materials, **do not just discard or dump these items.** Some may have decomposed to the extent that even moving or opening the stock bottles could present a serious toxicity or explosion hazard. Consult with professional hazardous waste experts such as those with your state environmental protection agencies.

This is not a list of all the chemicals that might be hazardous. The Merck Index, published and updated regularly by Merck and Company, Inc., is an excellent reference for determining the hazards of chemicals, as is the Flinn Scientific Catalog/Reference Manual, available at *www.flinnsci.com.*

Chemical Name	Chemical Formula	Possible Appearance	Outdated Use	Hazard— Comments
Ammonium dichromate	$(NH_4)_2Cr_2O_7$	Red-orange crystals	Demonstration volcanoes	Unstable; produces toxic by-products when burned
Benedict's solution		Blue liquid	Test for sugar	Caustic; not appropriate below high school level
Biological stains: Hematoxylin Safranin Methyl orange Methyl red	Various	Strong colors	Slide preparation	Many are dark permanent stains, difficult to remove from skin and clothing; some have been found to be toxic, carcinogenic, or teratogenic (causing malformations in embryos or fetuses of pregnant women); check latest information prior to use
Calcium carbide	CaC_2	Grayish-black lumps	Mixed with water to release acetylene	Fire and explosion hazard
Carbon tetrachloride	CCl_4	Clear, colorless liquid	Organic solvent	Poison by inhalation and skin absorption; carcinogen
Chlordane		Amber-colored liquid	Pesticide	Easily absorbed through skin and mucous membranes; highly toxic; EPA has banned from use
Chloroform	$CHCl_3$	Clear, colorless liquid	Anesthetic	Human inhalation can cause death; EPA lists as carcinogen
Colchicine	$C_{22}H_{25}NO_6$	Liquid	Preparation of mitotic slides	Highly toxic
Concentrated inorganic acids	(e.g., HNO_3, HCl, H_2SO_4, H_3PO_4)	Liquids	Various	Highly corrosive; some are volatile as well; serious burn and eye-damage hazard
Diethyl ether	$C_2H_5OC_2H_5$	Clear liquid (usually in a metal can)	Anesthetizing insects	Forms explosive peroxides slowly on exposure to air
Elemental mercury	Hg	Silver-colored liquid	Thermometers and barometers; illustration of density; electro-motive replace-ment demos	Highly toxic; absorbed through the skin; vapors readily absorbed via respiratory tract

Chemical Name	Chemical Formula	Possible Appearance	Outdated Use	Hazard— Comments
Elemental potassium	K		Demonstrate elements	Forms explosive oxides slowly on exposure to air
Elemental sodium	Na	Grayish non-uniform lumps	Explosive oxidation	Violent reaction with water releasing concentrated NaOH fumes and spray
Formaldehyde solution (also called formalin)	HCHO	Colorless clear or cloudy liquid	Preservative	Strong skin and mucous membrane irritant; carcinogen
Magnesium strips	Mg	Slim silvery coiled metal	Wicks for demo volcanoes; "sparklers"	Burns at very high temperature, releasing UV light that may damage eyes
Mineral talc	$Mg_3Si_4O_{10}(OH)_2$	Soft, white or gray mineral or white powder	Moh scale mineral; demonstration of cratering	May contain asbestos and cause respiratory problems
Picric acid	2,4,6-trinitrophenol	Clear to yellowish liquid	Specimen preservative	Unstable and explosive if allowed to dry to less than 10% water content
Potassium chlorate	$KClO_3$	White crystals	Generation of oxygen	Strong oxidizer that can cause violent reactions
Potassium cyanide	KCN	White granules or powder	Insect killing jars	Highly toxic; decomposes on exposure to air and moisture to produce deadly hydrogen cyanide gas; can be absorbed through skin or mucous membranes
Silver cyanide	AgCN	White or grayish powder	Silver plating; creating mirrored surfaces	Toxic; can be absorbed through skin or mucous membranes
Sodium hydroxide	NaOH	Small milky-colored pellets	Demonstration of exothermic reactions and acid/base experiments	Highly caustic; serious permanent eye-damage hazard from splash and fumes released during reactions
White phosphorous	P	White or yellowish waxy-looking sticks stored in water	Demonstrate spontaneous combustion	Spontaneous combustion; fire that is very difficult to extinguish; small particles remaining continue to reignite

Appendix B

NSTA Position Statement on Safety

Safety and School Science Instruction

Preamble

Inherent in many instructional settings including science is the potential for injury and possible litigation. These issues can be avoided or reduced by the proper application of a safety plan.

Rationale

High quality science instruction includes laboratory investigations, interactive or demonstration activities and field trips.

Declarations

The National Science Teachers Association recommends that school districts and teachers adhere to the following guidelines:

- School districts must adopt written safety standards, hazardous material management and disposal procedures for chemical and biological wastes. These procedures must meet or exceed the standards adopted by EPA, OSHA and/or appropriate state and local agencies.

- School authorities and teachers share the responsibility of establishing and maintaining safety standards.

- School authorities are responsible for providing safety equipment (i.e., fire extinguishers), personal protective equipment (i.e., eye wash stations, goggles), Material Safety Data Sheets and training appropriate for each science teaching situation.

- School authorities will inform teachers of the nature and limits of liability and tort insurance held by the school district.

- All science teachers must be involved in an established and on-going safety training program relative to the established safety procedures which is updated on an annual basis.

- Teachers shall be notified of individual student heath concerns.

- The maximum number of occupants in a laboratory teaching space shall be based on the following:

  1. the building and fire safety codes;

  2. occupancy load limits;

  3. design of the laboratory teaching facility;

  4. appropriate supervision and the special needs of students.

- Materials intended for human consumption shall not be permitted in any space used for hazardous chemicals and or materials.

- Students and parents will receive written notice of appropriate safety regulations to be followed in science instructional settings.

References

Section 1008.0 Occupant Load — BOCA National Building Code/1996

Section 10-1.7.0 Occupant Load — NFPA Life Safety Code 101-97

40 CFR 260-70 Resource Conservation and Recovery Act (RCRA)

29 CFR 1910.1200 Hazard Communication Standard (Right to Know Law)

29 CFR 1910.1450 Laboratory Standard , Part Q The Laboratory Standard (Chemical Hygiene Law)

National Research Council (1995). *Prudent Practices in the Laboratory*, National Academy Press.

Furr, K. Ed. (1995). *Handbook of Laboratory Safety*, 4th Ed. CRC Press.

Fleming, et al Eds. (1995). *Laboratory Safety*, 2nd Ed. ASM Press.

National Science Education Leadership Position Paper. (1997). Class size in laboratory rooms. *The Navigator.* 33(2).

Authors

George R. Hague, Jr., Chair, Science Safety Advisory Board, St. Mark's School of Texas, Dallas, TX 75230

Douglas Mandt, Immediate Past-Chair, Science Safety Advisory Board, Science Education Consultant, Edgewood, WA 98372

Dennis D. Bromley, Safety Instructor, Independent Contractor, Anchorage, AK 99502

Donna M. Brown, Radnor Township School District, Wayne, PA 19087

Frances S. Hess, Cooperstown H.S., Cooperstown, NY 13326

Lorraine Jones, Kirby H.S., Nashville, TN

William F. McComas, Director, NSTA District XVI, University of Southern California, Los Angeles, CA 90089

Kenneth Roy, Glastonbury Public Schools, Glastonbury, CT 06033

Linda D. Sinclair, South Carolina Department of Education, Columbia, SC 29201

Colette Skinner, Henderson, NV 89015

Olivia C. Swinton, Patricia Roberts Harris Education Center, Washington, D.C.

Nina Visconti-Phillips, Assistance & Resources Integrating Science Education (ARISE) Dayton, NJ 08810

—Adopted by the NSTA Board of Directors, July 2000

Appendix C

American Chemical Society Safety Guidelines

Chemical Safety for Teachers and Their Supervisors: Grades 7-12

The full text of the American Chemical Society's 32-page safety guide for grades 7–12 is available at *membership.acs.org/c/ccs/pubs/chemical_safety_manual.pdf*

Teachers can order single copies on request. For information, call ACS at 800-227-5558, e-mail *oss@acs.org,* or write Office of Society Services, American Chemical Society, 1155 16th Street, NW, Washington, DC 20036.

In the first section, "Safety in the Use and Handling of Hazardous Chemicals," the topics are Labels and Material Safety Data Sheets, Chemical Hazards, Eye Protection, Flammability, Corrosivity, Toxicity, Reactivity, and Physical Hazards.

In the second section, "Teaching Safety to Our Students and Other Safety Considerations," the topics are Risks versus Benefits, Accident/Incident Records, Insidious Hazards, and Safety Inspections.

In the third section, "Preparing Your Own Safety Checklist," the topics are Work Habits, Safety Wear, Facilities and Equipment, Purchase, Use, and Disposal of Chemicals, and Substitutions.

The fourth section is "A Commentary on Safety."

The guide also includes an introduction, a section for supervisors on how to use the guide, references, acknowledgments, and an index.

Index

Index

Index

Index

Index

National Science Teachers Association

Index

Index